WHEN THE EARTH WAS FLAT

The Black Moss Press Settlements series gives writers a creative non-fiction forum for focusing on their roots, the "place" out of which their writing has emerged, and the study of the craft itself.
Books in the Settlements series include:

The Farm On The Hill He Calls Home, by John B. Lee – #1
Calling The Wild, by Roger Hilles – #2
Riding On A Magpie Riff, by Richard Stevenson – #3
When The Earth Was Flat, Raymond Fraser – #4
Left Hand Horses, John B. Lee – #5
The Gargoyle's Left Ear, by Susan McMaster – #6

OTHER BOOKS BY RAYMOND FRASER

fiction
In A Cloud Of Dust And Smoke
Costa Blanca
Rum River
The Bannonbridge Musicians
The Struggle Outside
The Black Horse Tavern

biography
Todd Matchett: Confessions of a Young Criminal
The Fighting Fisherman: The Life Of Yvon Durelle

poetry
Before You're A Stranger
The More I Live
I've Laughed And Sung
Waiting For God's Angel

WHEN THE EARTH WAS FLAT

Remembering Leonard Cohen, Alden Nowlan, the Flat Earth Society, the King James monarchy hoax, the Montreal Story Tellers and other curious matters

Raymond Fraser

Black Moss Press
2007

Library and Archives Canada Cataloguing in Publication

Fraser, Raymond, 1941-
When the earth was flat / Raymond Fraser.

ISBN 978-0-88753-439-3

I. Title.

PS8561.R3W44 2007 C814'.54 C2007-904118-3

Cover photo: Marty Gervais
Design: Karen Veryle Monck

Black Moss Press is published at 2450 Byng Road, Windsor, Ontario, Canada N8W3E8. Black Moss books are distributed in Canada and the U.S. by LitDistco. All orders should be directed there.

Black Moss can be contacted on its website at www.blackmosspress.com.

Black Moss acknowledges the generous support for its publishing program from The Canada Council for the Arts and The Ontario Arts Council.

Le Conseil des Arts du Canada | The Canada Council for the Arts

ONTARIO ARTS COUNCIL
CONSEIL DES ARTS DE L'ONTARIO

ACKNOWLEDGMENTS

The author would like to thank the New Brunswick Arts Board for a grant awarded during the writing of this book.

Some of the pieces included here appeared first in the following publications: *Antigonish Review, Fiddlehead, Intercourse, Nashwaak Review, NB Ink, New Brunswick Reader, Pottersfield Portfolio* and *Weekend Magazine*. "The Guy In The Wings With His Pint" was originally published in *The Montreal Story Tellers* (Vehicule Press). Most have since been revised by the author.

CONTENTS

The Prince Of Fortara And The Flat Earth • 9
Royally Wronged • 15
Leonard Of Montreal • 24
The Climber • 37
Words • 44
The Guy In The Wings With His Pint • 52
The Larsen Boys • 74
Masks • 85
Hoofbeats In The Night • 92
My Ten Favourite Books • 98
Why I Sit On A Board • 101
Rex • 103
How Little It All Matters In The End • 108
The Curse Of Vera Petty • 112
Wolf Poses As Granny – Assaults Girl • 116
Ears and Other Parts • 123
Miracles • 125
The Tall Man • 129
The Hollywood Period • 131

THE PRINCE OF FORTARA AND THE FLAT EARTH

One day while I was visiting Windsor Castle the Prince of Fortara brought a curious incident to my attention. He had been leafing through a genealogy newsletter and happened upon a letter from Lord Louis Mountbatten concerning an article I had published in Weekend Magazine. The article, as I recall, was entitled *Royally Wronged,* and dealt with the case of one James Stewart of Blacks Harbour, New Brunswick, who claimed to be the rightful heir to the throne of England, Ireland, Scotland and France.

Lord Mountbatten mentioned showing my story to Queen Elizabeth II, and remarked that "the Queen was amused." Whether she said, "*We* are amused," can only be surmised, but I would hope she did. Since her ancestor, Queen Victoria, is best remembered for her statement, "We are *not* amused," the present queen might find a similarly memorable place in history for her own pithy comment.

Most people reading the above would not have a clue what I'm talking about, but it's a true story.

A man's home is his castle, and there are Windsor Castles and Windsor Castles. One is in England, which readers of the British tabloids are quite familiar with. Another is situated on Windsor Street, in Fredericton, and was for some years the residence of the Prince of Fortara, otherwise known as Alden Nowlan.

❖

Alden wasn't born a prince, any more than I was born the Duke of Northumberland. We both came from humble beginnings and had to go out into the world and acquire our titles.

Although my friendship with Alden covered twenty-two years, from 1961 to his death in 1983, what I know of his childhood I've learned mostly from his writings, and from dipping into some later (and not always reliable) biographies. Alden talked a good deal about his father, a rough hard-drinking man, but never once mentioned his mother, who abandoned him and his sister when they were quite young. It wasn't until many years after we met that I learned he had a sister. I still to this day couldn't tell you exactly where in Nova Scotia he came from. He called the place Desolation Creek – later Ketapasa Creek – and would say it in all seriousness, and that was as much as you could get out of him, drunk or sober.

❖

I began corresponding with Alden in 1961, but didn't meet him until a year later when another young writer, LeRoy Johnson, and I visited him in Hartland. I was sober on that occasion, and again on my last visits to Windsor Street in 1982 and 1983; but never during the intervening years. For all the nights I spent at his place I can't for the life of me remember what bed or couch I slept on. Claudine was always there, of course, brimming with life and good humour; and son Johnny at times, when he wasn't off to sea as a merchant mariner.

I'm not really sure what I can say about Alden in a few words (which is what I've allowed myself, so I won't put this off forever). His work speaks for itself and has only to be read to be appreciated. When I first wrote him back in 1961 — having seen his poetry in Fred Cogswell's Fiddlehead Magazine — I was twenty and living in my home town of Chatham, New Brunswick. By this time I was several years into my own writing and drinking careers. Alden replied and our correspondence eventually ran to 160 or so letters each.

We got together on a good many occasions over the years. As a veteran boozer from the Miramichi once observed, a man's got ten *good* years of drinking in him, and from then on it's all down hill. I'd say my ten good ones coincided with Alden's, from roughly the mid-sixties to the mid-seventies.

We had wonderfully lively parties in those days at Windsor Castle. Like one of his heroes, Samuel Johnson, Alden with a libation in hand was a brilliant conversationalist and story teller. It was unfortunate for the public he never found fame enough in his lifetime to become a feature personality on things like TV talk shows. It was also unfortunate he didn't have a sober Boswell around to record his monologues. The drinking nights were fun, but they had a way of dimming if not entirely erasing the memory.

It wasn't all one-sided at his house. There was frequently a spirited crowd around him, people who could keep the show going, a lot of give and take and flights of fancy. Alden's inseparable friend, the philosopher Leo Ferrari, was probably his most frequent guest, but visitors were always coming through the door, young poets and writers like Al Pittman, Louis Cormier, Bernell MacDonald, Jim Stewart, Eddie Clinton, Lindsay Buck, David Richards, Terry Crawford and Dave Butler. Also some older, long-time friends like Fred Cogswell and Bob Gibbs. And an assortment of army officers, politicians, newspaper editors, painters, musicians and what have you.

It was on one of these gatherings, in 1970, that the Flat Earth Society was formed. There were four of us in the living room that night, Alden, Leo, Sharon – my good wife of those days – and myself. I remember Alden and I playing with the concept of planoterrestrialism, and discovering (as might have been expected from two such radically progressive thinkers) that we were both sympathetic to the idea.

The philosophy of planoterrestrialism is too deep and extensive to go into here, so I'll merely say that after finding ourselves in accord, Alden turned to Leo Ferrari and said, "Leo, do you believe the earth is flat?" And without a second thought, Leo – who was discussing something with Sharon – turned and said, "Of course it's flat. Any fool can see that!"

Apparently it was an idea whose time had come, because before too many months had passed we were issuing tracts, had an irregular newsletter, and could boast a world-wide membership of close to two hundred. Alden wrote a story about the society for Weekend Magazine, and Leo – by now the FES President – became a much sought after speaker on the banquet circuit. My position was Chairman of the Board of Directors, while Alden – having his choice in the matter – adopted the title of Symposiarch.

❖

As fast as we were ascending in the world, we were to go even higher, when Alden discovered that the young poet, Jim Stewart, was most surely a descendant of the House of Stewart, the criminally deposed and rightful rulers of England, Ireland, Scotland and France.

We gathered a few hundred adherents there as well. With King James in a position to reward the faithful, the world quickly acquired a new aristocracy, with titles flying about left right and centre. Alden became Prince of Fortara, Leo the Archbishop of Canterbury, and myself the Duke of Northumberland and First Lord of the Admiralty. Everyone we knew and many we didn't were transformed overnight into Lords and Ladies of the realm.

And, as mentioned, when the usurper, Queen Elizabeth II, read my story about our movement, she affected to be amused. Not a word about her head's uneasy nights on the pillow.

There were bright times like the day Alden and Claudine and King James and Queen Jane came over to the Miramichi to inspect the Royal Navy. Before setting out to sea Alden christened the navy – my converted lobster boat, *Spanish Jack* – with a pint of Schooner beer, the champagne of the new nobility. It was no great decision deciding against the destruction of a good quart of wine.

❖

As everyone knows, a great many writers have been drinkers. Someone mentioned the other night that of the seven Americans who've won the Nobel Prize, six were alcoholics. The condition is not a disgrace, it's an affliction. In 1982 I reached the end of my own particular rope and began going to meetings, which got me off the stuff and so far has kept me that way.

Alden mentioned the subject in a number of his letters to me, and it was something we talked about from time to time. If nothing else, in his case, he had diabetes, and it's not a good idea for a diabetic to touch alcohol. He was aware of the problem but averse to the solution. He couldn't imagine himself giving up the bottle entirely, he said, pointing out that if it weren't for alcohol he'd never have had the nerve ask Claudine out, and so wouldn't be married to her now. As if he owed some kind of loyalty to the stuff.

The worst effect my drinking had on me was the loneliness I came to experience. People seem to disappear from your life, and if there are any still around they often don't want to have much to do with you – for good reasons – and you begin to think there is no one else like you in all the world. You can be in the midst of a hundred people and know that feeling. It's like an emptiness of the spirit, a lost and desperate feeling, a sense of total abandonment. It's what leads a great many drinkers to suicide, if something else doesn't get them first.

After I got sober Alden called me up a few times. Once he said he was out of gin and asked me to get him a bottle. I did, and found him in quite wretched shape when I got there, a condition I'd seen myself in often enough. He wasn't out of gin; he had half a dozen bottles in the cupboard; he just needed company. Another time it was for cigarettes, which he already had.

In one way and another, what I've mentioned can be found in his poetry, fiction, essays and letters. When I first wrote him, back in 1961, it was a fan letter. I was always in search of heroes, and saw one in him; then inevitably he proved a fellow mortal, and became something of real value, a friend.

He revealed a lot about himself in his writings, more than in person, and it's what I like most about his work. We get to know him there, and feel a kinship, see ourselves. It's the highest purpose of writing, in my opinion, linking one human spirit with another.

I was in Paris when Sharon wrote and told me Alden had died. I was still some years away from being able to cry but I got a tightness in the chest and a lump in the throat. I took a walk along the Seine thinking about him. I knew what I missed already, and it was to come to me different times after that. Alden was one of the rare people who *understood*. When something strikes you, and you think, Alden will know what I mean, and you look forward to telling him, knowing you're not going to get a blank look... And then you realize, well, I can't do that now. It's like losing a part of yourself.

Fredericton, 1996

(This is the article in Weekend Magazine that the Queen found amusing. It aroused a storm of letters-to-editors, as well as phone calls and correspondence to Dr. Nowlan, Dr. Ferrari, James Stewart and myself, some of them coming from as far off as England, Scotland, Ireland and the United States. Some were supporters of the cause and others were indignantly outraged by our audacity. Almost all were deadly serious.)

ROYALLY WRONGED

It is a sunny, late July day, and standing before the bow of a sea-going vessel which is about to be launched are three men. To the right, His Serene Highness, Alden, Prince of Fortara and Lord High Chancellor of the Realm. To the left, Raymond, Duke of Northumberland and First Lord of the Admiralty. And in the centre, in the tartan of the Royal House of Stewart, His Majesty James III, High King of All the Celts and King of England, Ireland, Scotland and France.

With kilt fluttering lightly in the breeze the King declares with regal aplomb: "We, James, by the Grace of God and for the Greater Glory of the Realm, do christen this flagship *Spanish Jack*." With a lusty swing he smashes a bottle of champagne against the ship's prow, and as the beverage sprays and foams a cheer goes up from the assemblage of nobles on hand to witness the event. The Duke and Duchess of Fogo are there... The Archbishop of Canterbury...The Duke of Dungarven and Lord Privy Seal...Baron Middleton... Sir David Breen... Lord David Murray Butler... Viscount Bernell MacDonald...

The date was July 25, 1973, and the place Chatham, New Brunswick. The ship, indeed the fleet, was my own 38-foot converted fishing boat, and the champagne a quart of Schooner beer. What was happening was not a mere pageant, however, a replaying of history during some summer festival, but the gathering of a real King and the Lords and Ladies of his Court.

It will almost certainly come as a surprise to most Canadians, and in particular those who consider themselves monarchists, to learn that the proper and legitimate sovereign of their country is not ensconced in Windsor Castle, or Buckingham Palace on certain occasions, but lives in New Brunswick. His name is James Stewart, descendant of the Royal House of Scotland, and he has mustered around him a considerable and vigorous following bent on restoring to him the crown of which his ancestors were deprived in the year 1688.

Knowledge of the existence of James III, claimant to the throne, came about through the diligent research of Dr. Alden Nowlan of Fredericton. Apart from being a well-known poet, playwright and novelist, Dr. Nowlan is one of Canada's foremost authorities on the royal houses of the world, and his special field is the study of the past and present reigning families of the British Isles.

In 1971 Dr. Nowlan was writer-in-residence at the University of New Brunswick in Fredericton and at that time James Stewart, a promising young poet, was a student there. It was a common practice for the younger writers to visit their mentor, and in the course of a conversation one evening Dr. Nowlan learned that James was not only born in Scotland, but that he was a descendant of the Duke of Albany, who was also the Earl of Fife. "But that goes back a long way and is of no use to me now," James told him.

Dr. Nowlan's interest was considerably aroused, however, and he decided to trace the young man's genealogy.

"It took me very little time to determine that here in New

Brunswick, in the person of James Stewart, was the rightful heir to the throne of England, Ireland, Scotland and France," Nowlan says. "I can explain why briefly, but first, because people are bound to wonder about it, I'd better straighten away the matter of the King's name. Why is it Stewart and not Stuart?

"Well, the last legitimate king of England was James 11, known as James Stuart. But this monarch was in fact of the Royal House of Scotland, the Royal Stewarts, who took their surname from the office of their ancestors, the High Stewards of Scotland, who came to the throne of Scotland through marriage.

"The ninth Stewart monarch, Mary Queen of Scots, decided for reasons not well known, to change the spelling. She had lived in France ever since she was a child, and no doubt it had something to do with the confusion of French and English spelling of names. But Stewart or Stuart, it's the same family. Besides, our James traces his direct line to an ancestor preceding Mary.

"We come to 1688 when James II, who was also James VII of Scotland, had his throne usurped. This resulted from his decision to have his first son, James Edward, baptized a Catholic, to the immense displeasure of a Protestant Parliament. In the face of all legality, they peremptorily exiled the King and his son to France and installed on the throne James's daughter Mary and her husband William of Orange, both Protestants.

"James II's son, James Edward, in his time naturally claimed the crown, as did his son in turn, Charles Edward, known as Bonnie Prince Charlie, but neither managed to regain it. The direct line of the family ended with the death in Rome of Henry Stuart, Cardinal York, only brother of Bonnie Prince Charlie.

"Thus, according to the divine tradition of direct line of succession – eldest son of the eldest son, and so on – the throne reverted to the heirs of the *second* son of the first Stewart King who ruled Scotland from 1371 to 1300, and this second eldest son was Robert, Earl of Fife. His eldest surviving male descendant and the rightful heir to the throne is James Alexander Stewart, our own James III.

"It's quite straightforward."

Once having established the lineage of James Stewart, says Dr. Nowlan, the only conscionable thing to do was to set about having him restored to his throne, provided, of course, he was not loath to take up the burden of the sceptre.

But that was not a problem. When informed of his legacy, the young monarch reacted quite calmly. "I'm a believer in Destiny. If King I am, then King I must be."

How this Restoration was to be brought about was a matter to be determined, but one thing was certain: a sovereign without liegemen is no sovereign at all. And since the old nobility of Great Britain could clearly not be considered, having pledged their allegiance to Elizabeth II, there was only one course to follow. A new nobility had to be created.

James III's first act as King was to invest Dr. Nowlan with the titles of Prince of Fortara, Duke of Wexford, and the office of Lord High Chancellor of the Realm, in effect, Prime Minister. To attend to the Spiritual direction of his subjects he appointed a new Archbishop of Canterbury, Dr. Leo Ferrari, professor of Philosophy at St Thomas University in Fredericton, and a leading authority on St. Augustine.

And since defence is always so vital to any state, and control of the sea so vital to the defence of Great Britain and her possessions, and since of all those in the King's immediate counsel I was most knowledgable of the sea, he made a third investiture. Hanging on the wall of my study is a document which reads:

> *We, James, by the Grace of God, King of England, Ireland, Scotland and France, do extend and give unto our beloved and most honourable cousin Raymond the title: Duke of Northumberland, Earl of the Miramichi, Baron of Black River and Office for the full extent of his life of First Lord of the Admiralty of the Royal Fleet.*

As the months passed the list of nobles grew. Invested with orders of the highest distinction were physicians, philosophers, painters, poets, soldiers, seamen, educators, thespians, theologians, musicians and agronomists, deserving men and women from all walks of life who were drawn by the justness of the young King's cause, among other reasons.

Aside from time-to-time meetings of the sovereign and members of the privy council, it was decreed by His Majesty that each year on September 21, the anniversary of the famous victory by Bonnie Prince Charlie over the English forces at Prestonpans in 1745, there was to be a gathering of the monarch and the peerage to commemorate past glories and to give liberal toasts to the coming Restoration.

This past year the celebration was held at the castle of the Lord High Chancellor; pipes and drums were on hand, and in attendance were upwards of a hundred of the King's faithful subjects, Lords and Ladies all.

Something should be said of the King himself, but it is difficult to do so under the circumstances. For one thing, royal security does not permit me to divulge too much information, since it might endanger His Majesty's person. And for another, while he's an eloquent man he is not excessively loquacious.

I requested that he give me a brief story of his life and he wrote simply: *James III. Born in Scotland in 1948. Has done a varied number of things.*

When I protested that that seemed insufficient, he took back the paper and wrote: *A King can write whatever he bloody well wants.*

It is known that he's a member of the Scottish National Party and is an accomplished musicians, playing half a dozen instruments; and like James I, the first Scottish King to rule England, he is a man of letters, being the author of two volumes of poetry.

Some years back, as though instinctively fearful of falling into the hands of the usurpers, he left Scotland and exiled himself in Canada.

It's a striking characteristic of the King that he accepted his new-found birthright, his prerogative to reign, so immediately and naturally, as though he had always known of it. There were no doubts or sudden affectations; his bearing remained what it had always been, modest but regal. To even the most jaundiced eye it was obvious that here was the stuff of a king.

The only conceivable objection to his rule, then, could not be his suitability for it, but the question of whether there ought to be a monarch in the first place, rather than an elected leader. For this is not a constitutional monarch, but an absolute one.

"Unlike a politician, the King cannot be bought and sold," points out the Duke of Dungarven and Lord Privy Seal, novelist David Adams Richards. "Nor does he have to assail the nation with lies and phony promises in order to get elected – his position is secure and inviolable. As King he need only attend to the well-being of the Realm, with the aid of responsible and sagacious advisers."

The Duke of Windsor, John Nowlan, a veteran of the Merchant Marine and more recently the First Sea Lord, feels logic is on the side of the young Pretender.

"Admittedly there have been bad kings," he says, "weak, vicious, indolent – even some congenital half-wits – history has had it's share of them; but our King James is a highly admirable man, and since the son is known by the father, as well as vice versa, it follows that the odds are in favour of the scions of the restored House of Stewart being worthy of the throne and beloved and cherished by their subjects. As our Lord High Chancellor, Alden, Prince of Fortara, puts it, 'The King is the human personification of the State, which is above politics. There is a dignity to a nation under the rule of a monarch, a nation not subjected to the spectacle of its leadership being repeatedly passed from one buffoon or scoundrel to the next.'"

The Duke of Fogo, poet and playwright Alphonsus J. Pittman, says, "I had no difficulty accepting my title and pledging fealty to the King. If one can accept the principle of hereditary monarchy – and in this crazy world, why not? – then it's just logical to side with the legitimate monarch. Besides, I can't see the other claimant to the throne granting me a dukedom, not to mention all the lands and privileges that go with the title, which I look forward to receiving after the Restoration."

Apart from the rightness of King James III's cause, and the philosophy of monarchism, his liegemen have other reasons for following his banner.

The Archbishop of Canterbury, for instance, states that, "In James

Stewart we behold the man born to be king, the man destined by fate to restore humanity to its rightful place in the scheme of things; also I expect to receive the beer monopoly once he is installed on the throne."

The Archbishop is a notorious home brewer and a forceful critic of the exorbitant taxes placed by elected governments on beer sold commercially.

"If this is democracy then why don't they get a specific mandate from the people to levy these taxes? They simply do it, knowing that if anyone protests he risks being labelled a drunkard. Shameless profits are made by governments off the poor toper, and this money is then thrown away on projects that the majority of the population either disapproves of or knows nothing about, until it's too late. The King's subjects will be happy to learn that I mean to remove all taxes from the sale of beer."

Artist Tom Forrestal, Baron Middleton and Painter-in-Ordinary (equivalent in painting to Poet Laureate) has received a special dispensation from the King to paint members of the Realm in the nude. The Lord High Chancellor reports that the Baron "has not made use of this, finding himself too shy to carry out said function successfully." Instead he has contented himself with adorning the Archbishop's mitre so that it may be adequately impressive on formal occasions.

With the King's following building up as it is, some reaction from the present occupant of the throne would seem a distinct possibility. "And it could be drastic," says the Lord High Chancellor, "since the other claimant's grounds for sovereignty are pretty shaky. There's a feeble sort of link between the Stewart House and that of the

Hanoverians, the Saxe-Coburg-Gotha family, or Windsors as they began calling themselves in 1917, but the connection is so thin it can't be taken seriously. This is a family of German and Sassenach origin, whereas James Stewart is descended from the Kings of All the Celts."

The King himself says: "I expect we'll all be arrested for sedition when this story appears."

Lord Glenburnie, the Baron of Bonne Bay, Gerald Squires, agrees that that could very well happen. "But it is more likely the world will be too busy chuckling at our grandiose titles to take us seriously. I can picture them: the Lords and Ladies of Great Britain, the Dukes and Earls, Barons, Bishops, the Knights of Columbus, the Supreme Commanders, Cardinals, Presidents and Chairmen-of-the-Boards, the Generals and Admirals and Chiefs of Staff, the Grand Potentates and Imperial Wizards and Magnificent and Glorious Grand Masters – everyone having a fine laugh at our titles."[1]

[1] I suppose I should mention that the majority of quotes attributed to the nobles and high churchmen in this article are not *perfectly* exact. They are reasonably close, certainly, but with a deadline to meet and no time to do interviews, I had to be content with imagining what those involved *would have said*, if I had actually talked to them. The written exchange with King James himself is, however, entirely accurate and (of course) legitimate. – *R.F.*

LEONARD OF MONTREAL

It took some doing, but I was able to pry Leonard Cohen's address out of Kenny Hertz. It was March of 1966 and he'd told me Cohen was back from Greece and living on Aylmer Street in downtown Montreal.

"Aylmer? That's my street!" I said.

"I know. It's why I mentioned it," he said.

"Where on Aylmer?"

"Why do you want to know?"

"Just curious."

A pause. "I don't think I'm supposed to tell."

"Why not?"

"I don't know. Maybe he doesn't want people barging in on him."

"I'm not going to barge in on him."

"Then why do you want to know where he lives?"

"Because you brought it up. You said he lives on my street and I'm curious where. If I said Henry Miller is living on your street wouldn't you ask me where? Wouldn't you want to know?"

"Well, probably."

"I'm not going to kidnap him," I said. "Irving Layton's address isn't a secret. My address isn't a secret. Yours isn't a secret. What makes Cohen so different? If you makes you feel better, I won't tell anyone you told me."

I suppose giving the address out lessened some of the special status that went with having it, like widening the inner circle. But he couldn't stand up to my logic and persistence. Being a young poet myself and one of the editors of Montreal's newest "little" magazine, *Intercourse,* I doubtless merited a foot in the door. It wasn't as if I were planning to sell him Fuller brushes.

Kenny himself had been an editor of another little magazine, *Cataract*, as well as of the little two-issue mag, *Tit 1* and *Tit 2*. Under the name K.V. Hertz he'd made something of a splash as a 16-year-old poet prodigy, but by the age of 17 his poetic flame had burnt out. He was still only nineteen or twenty years old at this time.

At any rate, next afternoon I bought a forty ounce bottle of Chateau Royale sherry for $1.35 and drank a third of it and went calling on Mr Cohen. It probably was a shade presumptuous, since I only knew him from having read a few of his poems and from the TV documentary film, *Ladies and Gentlemen, Mr Leonard Cohen*.

The day after my visit I recorded my impressions in my journal, as follows:

March 20, 1966. His apartment is a block and a half from mine, in an old greystone building at the upper end of Aylmer, near the McGill University football stadium. There are two apartments in the building and his is the one on the second floor. I rang the bell and he came down and opened the door and immediately ran up the stairs in his bare feet, gesturing for me to follow, like I was someone he already knew.

We were in the main room of the apartment, a combination living room, dining room and study. He obviously used the dining room table for his desk. There was a typewriter on it, and a portable record player, a full-sized tape recorder, a bundle of what appeared to be galley proofs, a telephone and a radio.

The radio was blasting some popular top-twenty song or other. He shut it off, and assured me I wasn't interrupting him, that he'd been working since early morning and needed a break. I asked him if he wrote with the radio on (it was almost full-volume), and he said he always did, it inspired him.

It wouldn't inspire me, I said. It would drive me crazy.

He's smaller than he looked in the film, his shoulders thin and his chest hollow, but his face is just the same, the ultimate poet's face.

As my reason for being there I showed him a copy of the first and so far only issue of *Intercourse*, and offered him a drink of wine. He refused the wine, drinking orange juice instead, but gave me a champagne glass for my own use.

As I filled the glass he asked me if I drank a bottle like that every day. I was tempted to say yes, not wanting to disappoint him, but admitted I didn't, not every day.[1] He said he wouldn't blame me if I did, because only a fool wouldn't go through life high if he could manage it. He wished he was a better drinker himself but all booze did for him was make him sleepy and stupid.

He leafed through my little literary magazine and complimented me on it, describing it as unique. Or to quote him exactly: "I don't believe I've seen one quite like it before."[2]

When I told him it sold for a quarter[3] he gave me a dollar, saying

[1] This was fairly early on in my drinking career (which ran from 1958 to 1982), before things started to get out of hand.

[2] I thought it was extremely handsome myself, well worth the work that had gone into it. My wife Sharon and co-editor Leroy Johnston and I had spent several days typing the master copy on paper stencils and cranking the pages out on an old prototype Roneo mimeograph machine and sorting and folding and stapling and so on. It was probably the worst-looking magazine ever produced anywhere, but at the time I didn't see it. I was like a doting parent with an ugly child, oblivious to its flaws.

[3] Today rare book dealers sell it for a hundred dollars a copy, when they can find one.

I could keep the extra seventy-five cents and send him the next three issues when they appeared.

Later on, after we'd talked a bit, he gave me another dollar as a donation to help the magazine out.

I was there the entire afternoon so we talked quite a lot. I'll jot down a few things as they come to mind. I remember him mentioning he'd never submitted poems to a magazine in his life, that editors always came to him first, which meant he'd never had a poem rejected. I told him that must be nice and I wished I could say the same for myself, having been rejected hundreds of times already in my young career. And then I had a bright idea.

"Since you mention it," I said, "about editors asking for poems and so on, what about giving us one for *Intercourse?* I mean if there's something you can spare. Maybe some old thing you have kicking around that you don't know what to do with and it's taking up space and getting in the way and – It doesn't have to be that great or anything."

He said he'd see what he had. He went to his typewriter, which had a big roll of paper inserted in it, like a roll of toilet paper, only wider and of better quality. It was evidently how he was doing his writing these days, after the manner of Jack Kerouac. He scrolled back through the roll, pausing now and then to read, and then stopped and took a pair of scissors and cut a small square out of the middle of the paper and passed it to me. On it was an untitled 12-line poem, which began like this:

Snow is falling.
There's a nude in my room.
She surveys the wine-colored carpet...

I read through it quickly and almost said, for a joke: "I'm sorry, I have to reject this." But good manners got the better of me.

In fact it wasn't one of his finer compositions, but I wasn't about to look a gift horse in the mouth. As I thanked him and tucked it in my pocket I was already seeing his name on the cover of issue number two, and thinking how it would help increase the number of our subscribers, which at present stood at none.[4]

As I said, I spent most of the afternoon with him, and probably did more talking than he did, being the one drinking the wine; but still I plied him with a good many questions. Some of his comments I found quite strange. For example, he said he considered books an obsolete form of entertainment and preferred watching television.

"Don't you find the commercials annoying?" I said.

"No. I especially like the commercials," he said. He called them a modern-day art form, like billboard advertisements – another popular art form. He said he enjoyed *everything* about modern North American life: television, movies, songs, dances, cars, planes, skyscrapers, neon lights. It was pop culture and he embraced it. "It's where the action is," he said. "It's what's happening."

Noting that *Intercourse* was subtitled "Contemporary Canadian Literature", he asked me what I thought of contemporary literature, whether Canadian or otherwise.

I said I didn't know quite how to answer such a sweeping question, and asked him for his opinion. He said it wasn't a very high

---

[4] The lino-cut cover of Intercourse II was created by the now well-known set designer Michael Eagen and hand-rolled individually by LeRoy Johnson and myself, all 500 copies! (Watching us Michael said we should change the name from *Intercourse* to *Handjob*). Cohen's name appeared on the cover, along with those of other luminaries such as Irving Layton, Raymond Souster and Elizabeth Brewster.

opinion. He didn't care much for what was known as "literature". All the traditional forms of imaginative writing were obsolete, he said. Films had taken their place, just as photography had replaced painting. Books were of little or no value and he rarely read them. Poetry above all was a dead art, pretty much useless as it was written now. The only real poetry of the past thirty years was in the lyrics of popular songs. And Bob Dylan was the best poet alive today.

I'm not so sure he really believes all of this. Some of it maybe, but not most of it. I'd like to think it's his defense against an unpalatable world, but more probably it's just an act. He was great in *Ladies and Gentlemen, Mr Leonard Cohen*, witty, mysterious, unpredictable; and on this afternoon I was his audience, and the show must go on.

Not that there's anything wrong with a good act. It's not on the same level with being genuine, but if done well, it's the next best thing.

He's thirty-one years old (seven years older than myself), and has four or five books published. He has new poems in that paper roll that's in his typewriter. In his film he said he was working on a second novel and writes six hours a day, and has lately begun making a living from it. And now he says books are of no value and poetry is dead?

Anyway, at this juncture the phone rang and he excused himself. I kept an ear cocked and gathered he was talking to a publisher about a manuscript he was in the midst of proofing.[5]

When he hung up he said, "Now what were we talking about?"

"You were telling me Bob Dylan is the best poet alive today."

---

[5] *Beautiful Losers*. Many Canadian critics consider it to be a "great Canadian novel", but I have to admit I fell asleep six or seven times trying to read it and finally gave up about half-way through. At the risk of offending people, it struck me as two hundred and fifty pages of quasi-poetical rhetoric (to use the polite term). Which is not to take anything away from Mr C's outstanding capabilities as a song-writer.

"So he is. His songs are poetry. Read them sometime. *The vagabond who's knocking at your door, is standing in the clothes that you once wore...* He's like the early bards and troubadours – he sings and people flock to listen. They fill halls by the thousands and buy his records by the millions. Isn't that how poetry should be? Isn't it preferable to the so-called poetry that bores students in the classrooms of English courses?"

"But you write poetry?"

"I write songs now."

"You do? I didn't know that."

He grinned. "Would you like to hear one?"

I could hardly say no. There was a guitar leaning against the wall, and he picked it up, and for the next half hour or so sang to me. The songs weren't short. There was one about a girl named Suzanne, and an even longer one called *The Stranger Song,* about "some Joseph looking for a manger", and four or five or six others. Once started he didn't want to stop. He wanted to make sure he gave me my money's worth.

He had a deep, sombre, rather monotonal voice, which to my ear sounded not too bad, in an unpolished folky sort of way. Although, to be truthful, I was more impressed by his guitar playing, since I've been trying to learn the instrument myself for a year or so and getting nowhere. And if I'm to be really truthful, I've yet to meet a man drinking who wants to sit for half an hour letting some other guy sing songs he's never heard before and which he can't join in on. But I kept my peace, and when he finished applauded his performance.

Then I offered to sing a while myself, as a return favour. I thought I would sing him some old Miramichi folk songs from my home province of New Brunswick.[6] He said he'd love to hear them, but

[6] I had moved from there to Montreal just the previous fall.

unfortunately had an appointment to keep. If I wanted to stick around, however, he'd listen to me when he got back. He would only be an hour or so.

As he was going out the door I said once again how much I'd enjoyed his film, especially the humour in it. "If you ever decide on a change of career," I said, "you could always become a comedian."

"I'm already a comedian," he said.

I sat for a while, and then got the idea to pass the time by recording some of the Miramichi songs on his tape machine. I wasn't concerned about how to operate it. By now I'd gone through about four-fifths of the wine and was confident I could master any piece of machinery.

There was already a tape in it. I pressed the play button and hearing Leonard's voice fast-forwarded and checked again, and did this until I was sure I wouldn't be recording over one of his songs. Then I started singing. I wasn't competent enough yet on the guitar to accompany myself, but I didn't let that bother me. The old lumberjacks who sang these songs never had accompaniment, and what was good enough for them was good enough for me.

The session went along quite well at the beginning. But then as I was moving through the fourth verse of that great doleful lumberman's ballad, *Peter Emberly,* I fumbled a line, and when I tried to redo it found I couldn't remember exactly how it went, and would need to think about it a minute. I shut the machine off and went through the song again in my head. The words came back, but now I had to rewind the machine a bit so I could sing over where I'd made the mistake. And this was where I got into trouble. I rewound back too far, then fast-forwarded too far ahead, then went back too far again. It was very hard to find the right place. I was jumping from stop to rewind to play to fast-forward to stop to I don't know what. And in my frustration I must have hit some buttons I shouldn't have, because Leonard was singing again and I didn't know if I was forward or backward and so I slammed a button and then another and suddenly the right reel stuck and the tape flew off and went flying all over the table and floor like a great string of confetti.

I had a hell of a time threading it around the reel again and getting it to look like it had never been touched. When I pressed "play" nothing happened. The same with the other buttons. I took a pull on my wine and finished the bottle off, and reflected that Leonard would likely be detained longer than he thought and so I might as well just leave, and the sooner the better.

❖

When I next saw him he didn't say anything about the tape recorder, and I saw no reason for bringing the subject up myself. Presumably he got the problem straightened out, and any songs he might have lost he would have recorded again. The extra practice no doubt did him good.

Where I ran into him was in a bar-cafe on Mountain Street one afternoon, a place called Le Bistro, or just the Bistro in English, where Montreal's literary and arty set hung out in the sixties. He was sitting by himself over a coffee and invited me to join him. "What are you drinking?" he asked. "You probably don't want a coffee."

"I think I'll have a Molson," I said.

"A pint or a quart?"

"Oh, I think I'll have a quart."

He insisted on treating me, and I didn't put up a fight. I had no income at the time (it was a few months before I landed a job as copy editor for the tabloid *Midnight*) and I knew he had an annuity from his late father's estate, which was why he could afford to live in Greece, as he'd been doing.

We chatted about one thing and another, and among other things I asked him if he'd been reading any good poetry lately. To me he was still a poet, no matter what he said. This notion about writing and singing songs – in the mid-sixties everyone was writing and singing songs, so I didn't think it was actually something he would take seriously.

"Only yours," he said.

"Really? You mean the ones in *Intercourse*?"

"Yes. And there was another I saw in *Talon*." Talon was a little magazine out of Vancouver, which I think had printed a poem of his as well. "I particularly liked that one."

"Speaking of which," I said, "I meant to ask you. Who's your favourite Canadian poet?"

Without a pause he said, "You are."

I laughed. I took it of course that he was being "original" and still working my vote. I wasn't laudably modest about my poetry, but I wasn't foolishly immodest either. I liked my poems, but at the time saw myself as potentially a better story writer and novelist.

I wrote the following lines about Cohen's comment some years later, in a poem called "The Cohen Endorsement":

I said Leonard who's your
favourite Canadian poet
and he said "you are"!

I told this to Seymour Mayne
who said no kidding (wishing it was him)
put that on your next book
my favourite Canadian poet says Cohen

except for witnesses
no third party just myself
nothing in writing no tape recorder playing
it would never stand up in court

a poem of mine he'd read
something about everyone's written everything
about everything and what's there left to write
and Irving Layton one day saying
the trouble with Leonard
he has nothing to say

It's true Irving Layton said that to me. It must have been hard for his ego to see his less talented (as a poet) protege (as Leonard had been) surpass him to such a degree in fame and fortune.

When we left the Bistro he offered me a drive home. I was living by this time out on Cote des Neiges Road, in another direction from his mother's house in Westmount, which was where he was headed. But he said it didn't matter and hailed a cab. As we turned onto Cote des Neiges and were climbing the hill he spotted a pretty girl hitchhiking and told the driver to pull over.

"Do you know her?" I said.

"No. But she needs a lift."

She had obviously never been offered a free ride by a taxi before and so was a little dubious, but seeing our charming faces she got in. As we motored along I informed her she was in the company of one Leonard Cohen, the famous poet and star of the motion picture, *Ladies and Gentlemen, Mr Leonard Cohen*. She seemed impressed enough by that, but what happened after I got out at my place and they drove off together I don't think I should say. It wouldn't be right, since I don't know.

❖

Later that year he went to New York and sang *Suzanne* over the phone to Judy Collins, and in December she released an album called "In My Life", which featured among other fine songs two of Cohen's, *Suzanne* and *Dress Rehearsal Rag*.

The following year, 1967, he released his own first album, and that fall I travelled to Dublin where I discovered that in Europe he had already become a famous songwriter/singer. In Dublin I met a young lady and bought the Judy Collins album for her and to this day the songs that are on it including Cohen's bring back poignant memories of those rambling days. We had been out a few times to the pubs before she found out I knew Leonard and from then on she would introduce me as Leonard Cohen's friend.

"Well, I wouldn't say we're *friends*, exactly," I'd have to qualify.

"But you know him? You've met him?"

"Oh yes."

"Bartender, give this man a drink! What's he like?"

❖

He reminds me of Bernard of Ventadour, a famous 12th century troubadour, who "like other troubadours was at once a composer and a poet; he created both the music and the lyrics for his songs."

C. Warren Hollister in his book, *Medieval Europe: A Short History*, writes: "At an early age Bernard showed great talent as a poet and musician, and was singled out by the Viscount of Ventadour for training as a troubadour. His happy days ended, however, when the viscount found the young boy in bed with the viscountess. He was banished from the castle and obliged to seek his fortune elsewhere."

Ever resourceful, young Bernard travelled to the court of Eleanor of Aquitaine, Queen of England, and sought an audition. Impressed by his gifts, the queen kept him around to compose and perform songs for her and her entourage.

Bernard's songs celebrate the joys and sorrows of romantic love, and became immensely popular, earning him fame and fortune, to say nothing of favours from the fair sex. Some forty of his compositions are still sung to this day, including such widely-known hits as *Lancan folhon bosc e jarric* and *Non es meravelha s'eu chan*.

Bernard of Ventadour afterwards joined the court of Raymond, count of Toulouse, and towards the end of his life retired to a monastery in southern France where he died.

Leonard at least for a while retired to a monastery in California, where he said he hoped to end his days.

With one thing and another, all these similarities, some tend to believe that in the 20th Century Bernard of Ventadour underwent a reincarnation, coming back for an encore as Leonard of Montreal.

THE CLIMBER

"How far you going, buddy?"

I told him Saint John, holding the door open and leaning in. He was a stocky little guy wearing wrap-around sunglasses and a work shirt with the collar turned jauntily up.

"Take you as far as Upper Blissfield."

"Okay. Every bit counts."

I climbed in and we drove off.

"You're lucky, fella," he said, shifting gears. "I don't pick up many hitchhikers these days."

"You don't?"

"Nope. I used to but not any more. Couple of years ago I'd never pass anyone on the road. Did a lot of hitchhiking myself once, I know what it's like... Hate to go by somebody, but..."

He took a pack of cigarettes from his shirt pocket and flipped it open. "Smoke?"

I took one and lit it. We followed the road out of town, passing the huge pulp mill with its mountains of logs and belching chimneys and reeking atmosphere. "Phew!" He rolled his window all the way up. "Don't know how people around here keep breathing." We crossed the Northwest Bridge and onto the highway leading to Upper Blissfield, and he said, "I picked up these two guys on the way to Moncton – that's my home, Moncton. They get in the car, couple of ordinary looking guys like yourself, but instead of getting in the front one of them jumps in the back. I don't like that, so I say to him, 'In the front, buddy, if you don't mind.' As I'm saying this I turn my head and almost get my eye poked out. He's holding a knife in front of my face. 'Start driving,' he says, 'and not too fast.' This is between Sussex and Moncton – you know that road? Well, anyway, I'm not real sure what to do, whether to take a chance and jump out and run or what. He's got the blade against my neck, I can feel it pricking. and he's nervous, he's shaking, so I figure I better do what he says before he shakes a little too much and slits my throat. So I drive."

He paused, dragging on his cigarette. "You see what can happen, eh? Not many like that, but some. They're the ones ruin things for all the decent guys on the road."

I waited for him to go on, but he didn't. Finally I had to ask, "What happened after that?"

"Nothing. They just wanted the car and my wallet. They waited till we come to a long stretch of woods and dumped me out and drove off. But it gave me something to think about, guys with knives like that. I flagged down the first car that came along, told the driver my situation, and we took off after them."

"You chased them?"

"Nope. This fellow I stopped, he didn't waste time either, a hundred, hundred and ten miles an hour all the way to Moncton, but we never saw hide nor hair of them."

"They must have turned off somewhere."

"Could be."

"Did you ever get your car back?"

"Yeah, what was left of it. Cops found it near the river, smashed into a parked truck. Pretty much a total wreck."

"What about the two guys?"

"Just disappeared. Them and my wallet."

"That's too bad."

"You're right." He glanced sidelong at me. "I just hope you're not that type of character yourself."

"Me? No, no. You don't have to worry about me."

"Wouldn't do you much good if you were. Tell you about another incident, happened only five or six months later. I had another car – brand new Buick. You might think I learned my lesson, eh? But some guys never learn. Well, I travel a lot in my line of work and it helps to have someone to talk to. Makes the time go by." He paused. "Any idea what I do?"

"No."

"I'm a climber, a high-tower man. The high jobs, TV towers, things like that, special work. Anything they want done away up there I'm the man they call."

"Sort of like a human fly?"

He smiled. "Yeah, something like that. A pretty good trade if you don't mind heights. Pays top dollar, you're your own boss, great hours. All you need is the nerves for it."

"I guess you would. It's not my style, I can tell you. I have nightmares about high places."

"Not many guys want to do it. It can get pretty windy up there at times. That's why I'm built the way I am. Look."

I looked at him.

"Not very wide but I got this thick chest. About two feet through. And arms. Look at these arms. That's from climbing, hanging on up there, takes a certain kind of strength. Upper body gets developed – maybe over-developed."

"I believe it."

"I was saying, about this other time. Lightning's not supposed to strike twice in the same place – but these two guys with the knife, you know, I didn't want to take it out on every hitchhiker. I never thought it would happen again. So here I am driving to Moncton one day, this time from Richibucto, on my way home after a job, and I see this young fellow on the side of the road, thumb out, he's holding a briefcase, wearing a sports jacket, a clean-cut looking guy. I figure he's a student maybe so I pull up, he gets in, seems polite and everything... We're driving along and I notice he's not saying too much, but that's no crime. About fifteen miles from Moncton he says, real sudden like, 'Pull over to the side of the road!' I look at him, I figure he wants to have a leak or something. But no, that's not it. He's got a *gun* in his hand. A revolver, and pointing it at me. And this one is shaking too – another nervous guy like the one with the knife. Sweat just pouring down his face.

"A man has his limits. One car just written off and now this jerk wants to play the game again. Well, I don't even think of the gun. I mean I should, but I say, 'Screw you, buddy,' and ram the gas pedal to the floor. It's a new Buick eight, right? not this piece of junk I'm driving now. These days I leave the Buick with my girlfriend. But at that time I was driving it, and it could move, believe me. She jumped into passing and we took off like a bat out of hell. I'd been doing about sixty before, in no big hurry, but now the speedometer leaped to ninety, then up to a hundred before the guy has a chance to think. He nearly got a whiplash neck out of it. His mouth drops open and he yells at me to stop, saying he's going to shoot, and for a second or two I'm just a little worried. But I keep her to the floor and we hit a hundred and twenty. 'Now listen, buddy,' I say to him, 'you pull that trigger and we're both dead, not just me. If this car goes out of control forget it, it's game over, curtains.' 'I'll shoot!' he says. So I say, 'Go ahead, you want to kill yourself that's your business.' I was putting it all on the line, I wasn't bluffing. The way I figured it, if I stop he's liable to let me have it anyway. At least this way I'll get a little of my own back. Anyway, it's the only weapon I got. I can be a pretty stubborn guy by times. I don't rile up easy but I had my fill of bozos high-jacking me and I was going to make sure this one regretted it, one way or another."

He stopped there, as though that was the end of the story. We were cruising along at sixty, passing fields and farms, white clapboard houses, stretches of woodland, a small sawmill with cones of sawdust and stacks of lumber. We rattled over a level railway crossing and started up a long hill.

"Well," I said at last. "What happened next?"

"Well," he said, "the guy gets in a panic, I can tell he's scared out of his wits, and he should be the way we're flying. A hundred and twenty on the turns. He's sure we're going to crack up, and a few times we come damn close to it. But I don't ease off and before long the guy's had enough, he can't take it, he starts whining at me to stop, he's holding onto his seat and begging me, he says he was only fooling and it was just a joke and would I please stop and let him out and we'd forget the whole thing. Some joke. 'Not a chance, buddy,' I tell him. 'I stop and you got the drop on me. Give me that gun first.' He wouldn't do it right away, he wanted to hang onto it. But in the meantime I'm ripping around bends on two wheels and passing on blind hills. On one stretch there was a car in front of us and one coming our way, but I wasn't about to slow down, so I passed on the shoulder side, and the dirt's flying everywhere and it looks like we're going to wrap around a hydro pole, but I get her straightened out. The guy just about shits himself. I glance at him and he's pale as a ghost. 'Okay, okay,' he says. 'Here.' He hands the gun over and I stick it in my belt."

There was another lengthy pause. I said, "Then what."

"Well, by now we're not all that far from Moncton, we're nearing the outskirts, so I slow down a bit, bring her down to eighty-five or so. I don't want to slow too much for fear this creep will jump out the door. I'm not about to let him get away if I can help it. I don't have too much to do with the cops but I figured this was one bird who should be kept off the roads. Who's to say what he might've done? That gun was loaded, it was no phony. Suppose I stopped when he told me to. Nothing there but woods. I might still be lying in the bushes with my head blown off. You never know. So I drove straight to the cop shop and took him by the scruff of the neck and lugged him in. And that was that."

I shook my head. "It's a wonder you still pick up hitchhikers."

"Yeah. I don't as much as I used to. I look pretty close now, study the faces. I'm taking a chance, but Hell, I hate to see the good guys have to pay – they still have to get where they're going and not everyone owns a car. Anyway, life's one big risk however you look at it, and you're going to catch it sooner or later. I risk my neck every time I go to work. Maybe I like it! I don't get bored that way."

When we reached Upper Blissfield he stopped at a service station and let me out. "This is as far as I go," he said.

"Thanks. It's a real help."

Upper Blissfield is a small place straddling the highway; the highway is its only street. There's a general store, a barber shop, the post office, a row of small frame houses, and an Irving's gas station. I walked on for fifty yards or so and stopped at a spot where I wasn't in front of somebody's front door and waited. A few cars and a loaded pulp truck went by. After a while a half-ton truck came out of the service station and stopped. The driver, a big-bellied ruddy-faced man, said he could take me as far as Boiestown. He grinned good-naturedly as I told him about my previous drive, the hair-raising experiences the guy had been through. "You must have seen him," I said. "He went into the Irving's after he let me off. A small guy with sunglasses."

"Oh, yeah. That would be Eddie Wormel. Wormhole, we call him. Well, he don't live in Moncton, he lives right there in Upper Blissfield, and the only climbing that boy ever done was up one of his mother's apple trees. He lives with the old lady and does some part-time janitor work at the school." He chuckled. "If anyone ever pulled a knife on our Wormhole he'd scare them off all right, he'd shit his pants. He used to shit himself all the time as a kid, and I can tell you from experience, it would scare anyone off."

WORDS

I date my friendship with Alden Nowlan from 1961 to his death in 1983, but there was a period of a year and a half or so when we weren't friends. I think I'll grab the bull by the horns and say something about that, for the record. It resulted from an incident in the fall of 1964 in Saint John. I'd just graduated with a BA from St. Thomas University in Chatham and taken a seventy-eight dollar a week teaching job at Belleisle Regional High School in King's County, about thirty miles from Saint John.

I was quite despondent when I got there. I'd been drunk the night before I caught the bus, and so was naturally low-spirited anyway, but when I reached the place it pretty well took the heart out of me. All I knew about Belleisle was the name, and – as anyone would who had a reading knowledge of French – expected to find myself on a *beautiful island*. But there was no island in sight, and no place to put one, even if there had been. There was a ditch running along the back of the farm house I'd been booked to board in, but it wasn't wide enough to hold a good-sized rock, much less an island. I was twenty-three years old and thirsting for excitement and adventure. I would have taken a job in Montreal or Toronto if I could have found one. But here I was, with nothing in sight except fields and cows and forest. My landlady, Mrs. Scovil (a lovely woman, but I didn't know that yet) was almost eighty years old, and the house – an old Wuthering Heights type of house – had been in her family for generations.

She showed me to my room and I set my bags down and fell to the floor sobbing. Or it's what I felt like doing. I was too much of a man to actually do it, but it was a near thing.

A whole year stretching ahead of me in the arse-end of nowhere, a place that God couldn't have found with a road map. I felt the walls pressing in on me. If I stayed here I'd be a basket case in a week – they'd have a deranged teacher on their hands, a menace to their children. They'd be sorry then they ever signed me to a contract. Putting visions in my head of sand dunes and palm trees and girls in grass skirts! I looked around wildly. There was no two ways about it. I had to make a run for it.

The Norton taxi had already left so the only way out was to hitchhike. I cursed myself for having brought so much luggage. I couldn't possibly sneak past Mrs. Scovil with three suitcases, an army duffel bag, a huge box of books and three packsacks, telling her I was going for a walk.

It was Saturday and school started on Monday. What should I do? I waited for a minute to go by, watching the second hand on my watch. A cow mooed and then all was silent. I decided to leave my luggage where it was and figure out how to get it later. I went downstairs and found Mrs. Scovil stirring a pot on a blackened wood stove and told her I was going to Saint John for the night.

"But you just got here. Your supper is almost ready."

"I have to see a friend. He's expecting me. I'll be back tomorrow."

Alden was working with the Telegraph-Journal at this time and living with his wife Claudine and son Johnny in a basement apartment in the north end of Saint John. I thumbed a ride in and gave him a call and we got drunk and I spent the night there.

The next day he gave me a drive to the edge of the outback, letting me off at Norton. I was still whingeing and whining about what I'd got myself into, and he must have got tired of it, because he said,

"Oh, come now, it's not all that bad."

"It's not?"

It was just a year, he said, and the thing to do was look on it as experience, something I might want to write about some day. And I could always get away every weekend. It wasn't as if I was in prison.

I needed someone to tell me that. I had a great deal of respect for Alden, and if he said it, then it might be so. I felt suddenly much better.

"You might actually like it," he said.

I'm not about to give an account of my year as a teacher, but it turned out to be less deadly than I expected. Another boarder was at Mrs. Scovil's on my return, a new teacher from Pakistan, and I came to enjoy his accounts of visiting the whores in Saint John ("Ah, Ray, I had the *best* of times!"). Mrs. Scovil herself was worth the price of admission, a Dickensian character in the flesh.

I recall her talking about her middle-aged son one day, in tones of fondly indulgent disapproval. "I'm afraid he's not as refined as he could be. Dear me, he gets so mad at the government. I remember they passed a law he didn't like and he said, "That's nothing but pure – " She paused, tittering. "Oh, I can't say it."

"What?" I said. "What did he say?"

"You know, like when a bull goes to the bathroom?"

I also liked the students, for the most part; there were some quite talented clowns among them. But I couldn't handle the rustic life on the weekends. I tried the first one to see what it was like and it wasn't like anything. Or to put it another way, it was like nothing. You can only gaze at hay for so long.

I bused in to Saint John the following Saturday for another stay with the Nowlans, and I'm not sure if it was then, or if it took another weekend after that, but whenever it was, I quite quickly wore out my welcome.

The way I looked at it, coming from the Miramichi, whether you were teaching or going to school or digging post holes for a living, you put your time in during the week and when the weekends came you got drunk, and that was life as the Almighty had ordained it.

What I didn't take into account was that Alden couldn't afford such a luxury – he needed his weekends for writing. It was all right for me, I figured I would teach for a year, taking a break from writing, and when the year was up something wonderful would happen, and I'd have lots of time and money, and could pen the immortal stuff to my hearts content. What miracle was to occur I didn't know, but I was young – eight years younger than Alden – and wonderfully optimistic. As for Alden, it would probably happen the same for him too, if he thought the way I did.

And that's about as much as I thought about it.

Alden didn't want to *tell* me I was interfering with his schedule – he couldn't, for fear it would hurt my feelings. If my feelings were hurt I might get mad at him, I mightn't like him. I can understand this sort of reasoning; in his place I'd probably have done exactly as he did.

What he did was start an argument. I didn't see it coming, I just thought he was growing a bit disputatious and contrary the more we drank, as drinkers sometimes will. But it got worse. In no time he was disagreeing with everything I said.

Thinking, well, we'll see how far this goes, I brought up the subject of Hitler, and immediately he told me what a fine man Hitler was, the only problem being people like myself who misunderstood him.

He went on and on in this vein, until I said, "That's preposterous. You don't really believe what you're saying about Hitler."

"And why not?"

"I don't think you believe half the stuff you've said tonight."

"Are you questioning my sincerity? Mr. Fraser, where I come from that's as good as calling a man a liar."

"You're telling me Hitler should have won the Nobel Peace Prize?"

"What I'm telling you, sir, is that I resent your questioning my sincerity. You come into my house and drink my wine and sit there smugly accusing me of..." And so on.

We were both quite drunk by this stage of the evening and neither of us was in a mood for backing off. I had no idea, really, what it was all about, but I wasn't too concerned, since in the condition I was in I just took it as a sort of verbal competition. As far as I could tell, I had all the easy arguments on my side. The only surprising thing was how personal he seemed to take it. In any case, the exchange went on until he abruptly got up and with a snarl went to bed.

I could hear him in the bedroom, talking loudly to Claudine. It's common knowledge that in a drunken state people tend towards delusions of grandeur. Alden was roaring, "I don't need this kind of shit! I'm Alden Nowlan, the greatest poet in Canada!" A pause. "No, Irving Layton's the greatest poet in Canada. I'm the *second* greatest poet in Canada!"

Whether he was the greatest or the second greatest, what he roared was indeed closer to the truth than a delusion, though he wouldn't have dreamt of maintaining such a thing sober. Irving Layton could proclaim his greatness, and Muhammad Ali, but Alden was from the

Maritimes, and Maritimers avoid that kind of thing. In one of his first letters to me he said he took a humble view of his talents, and at best might one day merit a footnote in the annals of Canadian literature. Obviously he's done much better than that, and will do better still, with time.[1]

Alden was still in bed when I left next day. I put our little skirmish down to the boozing getting out of hand. But when I returned to Saint John a week later and telephoned, Claudine informed me Alden was writing and couldn't be disturbed. And no, I shouldn't come over, because he'd be working all weekend. Yeah, but it's me, I said.

Well, me or no me, the way was barred. So I went and got drunk by myself and stayed with an aunt and uncle of mine who also lived in Saint John. I was quite burned up about it. I was the thin-skinned type anyway, and any kind of slight was like a kick in the belly. In this mood, and drunk to boot, I wrote Alden a crazed letter calling him all manner of things he wouldn't like. As far as I was concerned, we were friends no more, for life.

I did my year at Belleisle and moved up to Montreal and with a friend, LeRoy Johnson, started a literary magazine called *Intercourse* and got a job working for the tabloid newspaper, *Midnight*. And with the passage of time I cooled off. I never, through all this, stopped admiring Alden's writing, I just thought he'd taken a dislike to me and had been quite nasty in letting me know it. I still hadn't figured out the cause of his change of heart. We'd been good enough friends before that time; I still, in those days, while the going was good, got drunk with my friends every chance I could. And still assumed that's what friends did with themselves.

---

[1] *In vino veritas*. (A scholarly article like this would be naked without a Latin footnote.)

But old wounds heal, and night follows day, and spring follows winter, and I don't know what all else. I wasn't hanging onto bitter feelings. I was enjoying myself in Montreal, and wrote the incident off as just another idol fallen from the pedestal, which was always a good lesson in reality. It would have happened sooner or later, one way or another. The days when gods walked the earth were gone forever.

Since I haven't checked our correspondence – I'm not a meticulous scholar – I'm not sure why I sat down one day and wrote him. Most likely it was about then I heard he had cancer and thought I'd make the gesture. Whatever it was, he replied, and then sent some poems for the magazine, and we got back on track again.

I did, come to think of it, look through some of his letters a few months ago, before I knew I'd be writing this memoir, and was struck by how many times over the years he expressed his regret about what

had happened. He hadn't known how to mend the rift, and with his regard for friendships, I expect tormented himself about it.

Once when we were visiting him and Claudine in Fredericton, Sharon, my esteemed wife of those days, said, "You two get along so well. It's hard to imagine you ever had a falling out."

Alden thought a moment. "Oh," he said, "well, you know, we were quite young at the time. We're a lot more articulate now."

Which might seem an odd thing to say, if you didn't know that his father and mine had a good deal in common, including the incapacity to express what went on inside them. It was a tendency we recognized in ourselves as well, and something we both had to deal with.

Despite Sharon's remark, we did have a *few* more drunken disputes. But I found the way to get over them was to assume he wished they hadn't happened. I remember after one fierce debate calling him next afternoon and leaving a message on his answering machine. I said, "Al, don't worry about last night. It's bad enough being sick next morning without thinking you've made an enemy of a friend. We were both of us drunk and not in our right minds. So don't feel guilty and I won't either."

Claudine told me later he was very very grateful for that call.

As it happened, we never had another *big* argument, and only a few small ones, such as when I finally got off the bottle and brought him some AA pamphlets and he said I was worse than the Jehovah Witnesses and to get those damned pamphlets out of there before Claudine saw them. That was in the fall of 1982 and nine months later he was dead.

(Before the Montreal Story Tellers burst on the scene, fiction writers in Canada rarely if ever gave public readings of their work. The first in my experience to do so was the late Hugh Hood, who read at a Montreal literary night organized by Phil Desjardins and myself in 1969. Hugh had been griping about poets monopolising the limelight, and to let him know there wasn't a conspiracy – or if there was that we weren't part of it – we invited him to join the bill and read a piece of short fiction. Outside of Hugh's mind and some confabulations he had with John Metcalf, I think this was the germ of the Montreal Story Tellers.

The following memoir was written on various park and boardwalk benches in Nice, France, in 1983, seven months after I'd enroled in a well-known program listed near the front of the telephone directory. A good many years have passed since then, and while it hasn't been pure pleasure all the way, I was right in believing my imbibing days were behind me, at least to the present moment, somewhere in 2007.)

THE GUY IN THE WINGS WITH HIS PINT

I've never been particularly eager to re-read my finished writings, either privately or in public. Being a perfectionist of sorts I'm always afraid of running into some horrible flaw that's beyond my powers to correct. Nevertheless when Hugh Hood asked me early in 1971 to be one of the Montreal Story Teller Fiction Performance Group, as it was to be called, I said I would, thinking the public exposure might be what the doctor ordered. At the time I was approaching thirty and my career wasn't looking too rosy. I'd had a string of bad experiences and was frustrated and bitter. I felt the fates had set me up, because previously everything had appeared to be rolling along so well.

In the fall of 1969 Louis Dudek's press, Delta Canada, had published my third collection of poems (*I've Laughed and Sung Through the Whole Night Long Seen the Summer Sunrise in the Morning...*) and people seemed to like it, for the most part. Then in February 1970 Chateau Books accepted my latest version of a novel (*The Robin Hood Gang*) and I signed my first contract with a publisher. Shortly after that I completed the rough draft of another novel. And in April I received a Canada Council grant.

The day I got the grant was my idea of how a typical day in my earthly kingdom should be. The sun happened to be shining, and I left the post office and strolled the streets of downtown Montreal like a being in a higher dimension than the poor mortals I passed. In my foolish rapture I wondered if those dreary unfortunates could detect by the radiance on my face what a lucky chap was I. I wanted to tell them all, grab them by the lapels and say, "Guess what I just got?" I was filled with a sense of unlimited freedom, a multitude of desirable choices open before me. It was the first time in my life I'd had a substantial sum of money (the grant was $3,500 plus return fare to Europe) and it was *all free*... which meant I could spend it as I pleased without feeling guilty. For a fellow with my background, where the pennies were always watched, this was a delicious sensation. I even delayed going to the tavern because it didn't make sense to drink; how could I improve on the high I already had? There would be something morally wrong in drinking now, no excuse for it; and so I put it off for a half hour. Later I bought a big steamer trunk at a second-hand store (I couldn't lose my habit of frugality all at once) and a tent and sleeping bags and rucksacks and champagne and four or five other kinds of fancy wine. First the celebration then so long, Montreal, time to move on. Not that I'd been unhappy the past few years in Montreal, I hadn't, they'd been good years; but there was *more* to be had, more of life's delights.

It seemed clear to me that my train to glory was on the rails and commencing to build up a head of steam. I'd been earning a reasonable living writing for tabloid newspapers (*Midnight, National Examiner, National Spotlite,* etc.), but now I was free to quit this demeaning occupation. My wife Sharon and I packed our stuff and departed for Newfoundland for a summer of camping on Little Bonne Bay Pond with our friends Al and Marilee Pittman. And from there we flew to Spain. Spain in September was like Heaven. The hot sun and the clear emerald Mediterranean, palm trees and walnut groves – writing and swimming and eating out every night, and the booze so cheap it was almost free. Sixty cents for a litre of brandy – like that. A gargler's paradise, as Brendan Behan called it. But my drinking was negligible. I'd work in the morning from eight-thirty to twelve, walk to the beach for a swim and a snack, then back to work until four or five. And only then would I open a beer. It's true that once started I drank steadily until eleven or so, but leisurely. I not only didn't get drunk but didn't want to. I didn't need booze – I was content by my standards, I had things my way. I was pretty sure I did. There were moments of doubt, admittedly, since not *everything* was in the bag. I was impatient by nature, and tended to create concerns if none were at hand. Until my new novel was actually out and on the shelves I couldn't be in a state of perfect relaxation. But working during the day and nine or ten beers and a half litre of wine in the evening kept me fairly tranquil. Most likely my novel would be a spectacular seller and there'd be wild bidding for the new one. Movie offers, the problems of fame. For the most part I viewed my prospects with complacency, borrowing emotional charges on my future winnings. I practised affecting a personable modesty, which wouldn't prevent me from pronouncing on and straightening out a certain number of unwarranted reputations, should anyone ask.

What actually came to pass, and in a quite short period of time, was altogether different.

First of all, Chateau Books had a change of heart about my novel, and following assorted inane proposals ("Why don't you try re-writing it into something like *Love Story*, that's what's selling now") they reneged on our contract and returned the manuscript. Then the new book I'd finished in Spain and submitted to three publishers at once was rejected by all three within days of one another. And a week later I was informed by the Canada Council that they weren't renewing my grant. Winter was here and instead of the beaches and cafes of Spain I was grumbling about in an apartment I despised in cold Montreal. My literary magazine, *Intercourse*, which I'd handed over to a poet friend to publish, got into the hands of Tyndale Martin and his pseudo-Buddhist cult and appeared as the voice of The Great Heart Monastery, which was a far cry from how I'd conceived the thing. I added that to my list of reasons for feeling badly done upon. I was too proud to go back to the tabloids (I'd told them goodbye for good) so I had no paying work. And then NOISE started to really get to me. For a long time I'd been abnormally sensitive to noises, annoyed by them, and often with justifiable reason, but now they began to drive me completely loony. It was probably a case of something definable to focus my anger on – an anger brought on by frustration and apprehension. I was being threatened with failure, and it scared me. I'd been accustomed to take eventual success for granted. I saw myself blossoming in a certain way, and if it didn't come about, what was I then? The world would be severely disappointed in me. I'd have let billions of people down, the dead as well as the living, and those yet to come. The weight of so much disapproval was horrible to contemplate. I could hardly maintain I was doing everything right if I hadn't the credentials to back me up. The way things were now, and after all the time I'd been at it, could I even call myself a writer? A few books of poetry – what were they? With all that extra white space on the pages...

The blueprint in my head and the reality beyond weren't jibing, which is a common starting point for lunacy, in radical cases. Some manage to alter their vision, others try and shape the world to fit it – like the characters in my novel *The Struggle Outside* (plug). And others let themselves be eaten away inside.

I was already a dedicated tippler at this time. I couldn't stray far from the bottle. I drank every day to feel a human among humans, to ease pressures, face obligations, diminish fears, magnify pleasures, stifle guilts, lessen pains... trying to outwit the dealer, in other words. I had developed a considerable tolerance for the stuff and rarely got noticeably drunk, and might have maybe a couple of serious hangovers a year. I thought I'd found the secret to successful drinking. But the recent turn of events had put me into such a dismal state that sobriety wasn't merely uncomfortable, it was intolerable. I was morose and enraged by turns – those were my two moods, my unfailing companions; always one or the other, until I got sufficiently oiled.

Every few days I'd go across the street to a small grocery store for my supply of beer. I was amused when the young fellow who worked there said, "Man, you must have a hollow leg!" The owner of the store asked me one day what I did for a living. I said, "I'm self-employed."

He nodded knowingly. "Well, that's all right, I don't knock it. I'd rather work myself but each to his own. You can't blame a guy for taking it if it's there." He obviously thought I was a welfare drunk, or something of the sort. But I had nothing to come back with. I was eking out the last of my grant money, and just about all I did was drink.

I didn't write anything to speak of for about eight months. I'd sit at my desk and say what's the use? blaming publishers and editors and the universe. I'd written five unpublished novels in ten years. Why do another one? Why do anything? Maybe I had no talent and had been deluding myself all this time. The possibility made my stomach turn. It was an idea I didn't dare entertain. If I was mistaken there, in something that essential, then I couldn't trust myself in anything. Moreover I hadn't left myself an option to fall back on, all my eggs were in the one basket. So every day I sat around feeling lousy and guzzling beer to change the picture.

That's how I was during most of my time with the Story Teller troupe. So far as I could see the show biz angle was the only thing I had going. But I often felt like a charlatan, pretending to all those people out there that I was a flourishing author.

And I had to wonder about the other guys, what they thought I was doing with them. To myself anyway I was the odd fellow of the five. The rest of them had their fiction in books. They all taught English Literature for a living. None of them was a poet or a practising drunk. I was not included like the others in the anthologies of stories John Metcalf was editing, and felt kind of uncomfortable when they'd discuss these collections as if I wasn't present. I had the sense of being one of them by accident or mistake. Perhaps I helped make the group unclassifiable, visible evidence that we were an assortment of varied individuals and not a "school," a tag each of us was quick to discredit, being jealous of our unique identities.

The fact was, obsessed as I'd been with writing novels I hadn't written very many short stories. And the novels weren't such hot stuff either. Before long I'd cranked out another, making six in all by the age of thirty, and basically I didn't know what I was doing; it was as simple as that. I wasn't ready, but I was impatient, so I did the things anyway. One I completed in two weeks, 250 pages. The others took no longer than four months. I didn't want to strain myself. I wanted the finished product to come easily. It was only later I learned to take pains.

As for performing, I thought that for anyone to stand on a stage and read to an audience he would have to be half-pissed. It surpassed my comprehension that this evidently wasn't true for the others, for Clark Blaise, Hugh Hood, John Metcalf, and Ray Smith (to get their names in here... in alphabetical order). I couldn't understand it. I had to conclude it was because they were all teachers and used to lecturing and reading in front of students. I wasn't. I always packed a pint of rum or brandy and settled the butterflies before I went on.

Of the stories I did have in stock, maybe only a couple were sufficiently free of vulgarities and crudities to be fit for reading to high school students, who comprised most of our audiences. But with a few exceptions (which I saved for the universities and general public) I read them anyway. I thought they might prove entertaining, and if I had any honourable idea about the Story Teller group it was to demonstrate to students that literature could be enjoyed as well as suffered as a course of study.

It goes without saying that all five of us wanted to make a good showing, to please the crowd. We weren't above aiming for a laugh, because when you give these readings and people just sit staring you can't tell if you're getting anything across; but laughter is an unmistakeable reaction. And sometimes there were other reactions.

About the only thing I wrote in my arid period was a story called "Spanish Jack." I'd originally composed it as a newspaper feature and sold it to one of the tabloids. My partner in crime in those days, a photographer, had got hold of a large collection of European medical and wire service photos, and once a week we'd sift through them looking for ideas. We came upon one of an elderly lady who'd had a breast removed surgically, and we matched her up with a bewhiskered old bum in a seaman's cap with a cigar butt in his mouth... *Sex-crazed Man, 76, Bites Off Wife's Breast.*

One day, looking through my collected tabloid works, I thought, now I wonder if I can take this crazy tale and make a short story out of it. Because it was a fact that many of the wild yarns I used to invent for the tabloids sooner or later had their real-life counterparts show up in what's called the legitimate press – which is to say, there's almost nothing you can invent that someone's not going to do somewhere in the world, or hasn't already done. I wrote "Spanish Jack" in a folksy down-east kind of style, and when I used it at a couple of readings everything rolled along quite amusingly, the audience chuckling and grinning, until I got to the *piece de résistance* where the old chap clamps his teeth onto the missus's breast and bites it off and spits it out on the floor. Well, there was no laughter, but rather a mass retching sound, a vocal consensus of disgust.

I read the story at Sir George Williams and later at the University of New Brunswick in Fredericton, where Alden Nowlan (God rest him) came to the reading. I was second or third on the bill, and he got up and left after my bit, and everyone said, "Alden was so revolted he walked out." But that wasn't so. We were longtime friends and he afterwards assured me that he'd only come to catch my act and when I was finished he left. In fact I stayed at his place that night. The truth is he thought the tale was gross but not enough to drive him from the room.

The first time I read it Ray Smith said to me, "Fraser, you don't refer to a man's penis as his 'knob' in your narration. In the dialogue, okay, maybe, but in the *narration*, for God's sake."

But my narrator was a character, too, so he could call a penis anything he felt like. My narrator is almost always a character. I have to first invent someone to tell the story. I need a consistent attitude, that's the thing, and I don't have (at least up till now) enough idea who I am to use myself personally.

I enjoyed hearing the other guys read. Maybe I was wrong, but for the most part considered them better public readers than myself. I hadn't a clue what I was doing, how to use my voice – modulation, intonation, emphasis, whatever it's all about.[1] I was surprised, however, that my fellow stars – with the exception of Hugh – would read the same couple of stories over and over. I remember how it disappointed me to learn that comedians performed night after night the one routine, and singers did a set pattern of songs and patter, and politicians delivered the identical speech in different cities. I thought one was obligated to give an original show each time, in case someone was in the audience twice – or for the benefit of the rest of the cast. This was naive on my part, I realize now; but I expected performers to be always spontaneous and original, nothing rehearsed, no tricks,

[1] See "Afterword" for a later observation on this subject.

no gimmicks. Ideally – and for a while – I believed a writer shouldn't revise his work, that to do so betrayed the concept of pure inspiration. I had lots of good ideas in my time.

At all events I tried for a while to read something different every show, and it wasn't easy, because my supply at first was limited. I was forced to use some dubious material: for example a parody of the *High Noon* type of movie. One of the kids during the question period after asked me if I only wrote cowboy stories. I had trouble explaining what I'd done, since the youth had taken my story seriously, but I was rescued by Clark Blaise stepping in and lucidly explaining my intent. It was remarkable how my companions could talk on the subject of literature. I rarely talked, about anything (or so I seem to recall). I couldn't be bothered. I saw talk as a dissipation of vital energy, and to tell a story vocally as wasting it on a limited audience. I later took to drunken raving, but it was only later still, when I sobered up, that I began discovering how to open my mouth. I've found it's good for me, and I don't mind repeating my stories either. I've been a slow learner in more ways than one.

I had my little successes. One of my stories, "The Newbridge Sighting," required that I do an unusual voice for the principal character. He was based on a person I knew and I could bring him off fairly well, I think. After the performance a teacher asked me if I'd ever considered taking up acting. It wasn't meant as an insult or a hint: he confided that he thought my story had gone over the best of the lot. But me, an actor? I'd never been so flattered. Even in my drunken fantasies I only barely thought I could be an actor. I was the reverse of the type, as I conceived it – self-conscious, nervous, fearful of crowds, outwardly unemotional. Of course with a quantity of rum in me performing wasn't that hard – I might even say I enjoyed my stage appearances, especially if there was a microphone to give me a big voice. But you weren't getting the real me. It was always painful when sober to run into people I'd first met while drinking. I didn't like them to find me out, that I wasn't the free-and-easy chap I'd passed myself off as.

In April 1971 Sharon and I moved from Notre Dame de Grace where the nearest tavern was a mile away (I hated that neighbourhood) to a tiny apartment on Esplanade, at the back of a building. She had a part-time nursing job and I was making forty dollars a shot from our readings, and we paid eighty-five dollars a month rent, with furniture, heat, and electricity included. It was called an apartment but it was no more than a medium-sized room partitioned into a bedroom, living room, kitchen, and bathroom. I remember visitors staying with us, and how when we opened the living room couch out to make a bed it filled the whole room – you stepped through the door and onto the bed and that was it.

There was one school where I must have given an inspired performance, because I sold about thirty copies of my poetry book *The More I Live* after the reading. I was always the one who sold books, mainly because mine had a tag of fifty cents, while the other guys had novels and story collections that were beyond the means of the students. At this school they had their own literary magazine and they wanted to tape an interview with me and print it. I have a feeling they could sense I was emotionally about their age, therefore easier to approach. I said, "Sure, come and see me anytime." Seven or eight of them did show up one day and it was quite a feat packing them all in, like cramming a football team into an elevator. I produced a big pitcher of homemade beer – with the volume I drank that's all I could afford by this time, brewing it at a cost of seven cents a quart – and poured around, and kept refilling the pitcher as the interview proceeded. When we finished an hour later the youth handling the tape recorder discovered he'd pressed a wrong button and not a word had got taped. But I don't think they cared, they didn't appear to, anyway.

I'd read several issues of their magazine, and some of those youngsters had writing talent. But I suspect I dampened their literary ambitions. Because here was I, one of the famous Montreal Story Tellers, and here was the hovel I lived in. I'd noticed the expressions on their faces as they walked in the door, the dismay with which they parted the cobwebs and booted the cockroaches aside, slipping on the mud floor, huddling their coats about them as the wind whistled through the cracks in the wall. Or had the cockroaches been lately exterminated? I can't remember.

But a few writers more or less, what's the difference? There's no shortage of potential talent around. I saw quite a lot of it when I edited *Intercourse*, young writers with ability to burn; but they'd come and go, they didn't stick with it, they must have found better things to do. There was something missing, the obsession, the need, some factor that precluded their making a full commitment. I've thought at times they merely got wise. But I don't know.

Had I been one of those kids maybe I'd have found an element of romance about how Raymond Fraser was living. I was in favour of fame and riches and so forth, but my daydreams weren't consistent. I also saw myself as a Henry Miller type, living it rough and in disregard of conventional symbols of success (although of course still getting my books published – that was the *sine qua non*). And after I tired of this role I could shift into the yacht in Antibes and apartments in Paris and Rome and affairs with movie actresses and all sorts of interesting diversions.

But being where I was, and with no guarantee it was the early part of an eventually happy biography, I was bitter about my lot. For all I knew my condition wasn't going to get any better. And because I was me, life owed me more, there were no two ways about it. So what was going on around here?

One of the reasons I was so sensitive to noise had to be because my daily heavy drinking put my nerves on edge. But physiology aside, I was incensed that my sacred privacy was being invaded, I was being bombarded and assaulted by that rotten world out there. It was an indication of humanity treating me with indifference, offending me and neither knowing nor caring; an inimical chaos deaf to my complaints – first my orders, then my complaints, and what next, my berserk screams of impotent rage? Something of the kind. Like crossing the street in a crowd and a taxi nosing round the corner blasts its horn and I kick the door of the car and yell, "*You lousy goddamned bastard! FUCK OFF!*" The other pedestrians moving quickly away... a maniac loose on the streets...

Every Saturday there were weddings, and lines of cars would stream by on Park Avenue and St. Urbain Street with the drivers leaning on their horns. I actually picked up the phone several times to call the cops in order to lodge a complaint. But with phone in hand I realized they'd just think I was nuts. "Some crackpot wants us to stop all the weddings in the city." One day a helicopter landed in the park which faces Esplanade; it made a hell of a racket coming down, and again I was about to summon the law – it was all I could think of, my only recourse – when I saw it was a police helicopter. What do you do then?

I got into such fits that I felt I needed to retaliate. When I lived in NDG I used to daydream of getting a rifle and firing at the jetliners that flew low overhead in their approach to Dorval. There was a dog that barked every day on a nearby balcony. I wanted to shoot him too. I'd pace the floor and kick the walls. One day when the traffic seemed particularly bad I raced out the door on Esplanade and strode the length of the block snapping off all the aerials on the cars parked along the street. That would show them.

This was a little later on, early in 1972. A year before that I organized a march on City Hall to protest against the tyranny of automobiles in Montreal. There were some sane people took part in this… it was rather the thing at the time. I got into it in the way I involved myself in a number of escapades, while I was three-quarters crocked. A lot of talk, and next day I discovered I'd been taken at my word, and to save face (I always honoured my drunken commitments – I was too proud not to) I found myself in the police station procuring a marching permit. I talked to an assistant chief inspector. He was a calm, fiftyish man, friendly and civilized, a personable executive sort. I felt like an idealistic adolescent in front of him, and I was surprised he took me seriously, or pretended to, and didn't just show me the door. I was hoping he would, because all I could think of was getting to the nearest tavern. It was morning and I'd come into the station with only a few pints of beer in my belly. I really did feel like a fool, some kind of woolly-minded idealist, a dilettante of life, conscious of being graciously tolerated by a man who had important practical matters to deal with. He asked me my occupation and I said I was a writer. He was interested. He said he liked to read, and what had I written? I told him I had a novel coming out soon, in a few months probably. He said he'd be sure and look for it. I hope he didn't look too hard. That's the type of thing I mean. It was humiliating to have to lie to people.

Finally I got the permit and a couple of mornings later at the scheduled hour the march got under way – in the worst snowstorm of the winter. About a dozen people turned up with placards condemning traffic noise and air pollution and cross-town highways wrecking neighbourhoods, and with an escort of police motorcycles – as many of them as us, just about – we leaned into the driving storm up to our knees in snow, barely able to see one another, plowing along from Philips Square to Old Montreal. The whole scene was ludicrous, a fiasco; it was so ridiculous I couldn't help laughing. I was thankful there were few people out-of-doors to see us. For a climax someone stuck a leaflet in the snow on the steps of City Hall and then we all headed for a nearby bar. Even years later in recalling that experience I'd find myself wincing with embarrassment.

It was during this time that I gave up writing poems.[2] I stopped when the panic set in. Writing for fun wouldn't do any longer, I had to get serious, efficient. Turning thirty made a strong impression on me. I got to worrying about the future. I couldn't stay "promising" forever. I had to concentrate my energies and get some hard results. And yet I didn't seem to have any energies. I was in a defeatist stage. But I eventually decided I'd better do something – after eight idle months – if only to keep myself occupied. Thus it was that like a worn-out old man I set myself to write a sixth novel. I kept at it almost every day over the summer months, typing words onto pages, but it was a worthless dispirited effort, I'm sure the worst writing I did in my entire life.

---

[2] Well, not entirely. I continued to write *some* over the years, and in 2000 put out a "new & selected" (*Before You're A Stranger*, Lion's head Press).

I later read it through and saved two sentences out of 75,000 words and threw the rest in the garbage.

Meanwhile Hugh Hood was having his latest book published by Oberon, and he informed me that Michael Macklem, the publisher, was interested in my work... he'd personally liked my novel manuscript *The Robin Hood Gang*, even though he'd rejected it on the advice of others. He told Hugh he'd like to see a collection of my stories. I wrote Macklem and got back a nice encouraging letter. Encouragement was just what I needed. So what if I didn't have enough good stories for a book? I soon would have, just watch.

I sat down and in a couple of months wrote "The Quebec Prison," "They Come Here to Die," "On the Bus," "A Cold Frosty Morning," and "The Janitor's Wife"; and adding some earlier things and titling the lot *The Black Horse Tavern* I put them in the mail.

And in a while they came back. Rejected again. If I was in a bad state before, and I mean by my reckoning, my crazy inner world, it was mild to how I felt now – because while I was never sure about the other works, I *knew* this was a good book. It was the best I was capable of right then. I hadn't been lazy or self-indulgent, I'd taken my time and revised carefully and objectively. This time I was right for sure, and *they* were wrong. So after all it wasn't me – it really *was* them. That was more than disheartening, it was scary. If I was right and everyone else was wrong, that meant in effect that I was wrong – my entire perception was out of whack, my standards meaningless. To double-check I sent the manuscript to Doubleday, and got another rejection. The hell with it.

I wasn't going to throw in the towel, I was too stubborn; but what could I do? A violent frenzy seethed inside me. I couldn't stand it. Naturally I had to drink – if I didn't thoroughly anaesthetize myself I might do something catastrophic. Every day I sat at the kitchen table guzzling beer and going over in my head how I could rob a bank. If I had money... with money I could start a publishing house, put my own books out. I didn't know how to get money any other way. I cased the banks, outlined getaway routes, dreamt up disguises – I worked it out in detail, all the fine points, the plan getting thorough and elaborate. But what if I got caught? I doubted I could handle a long stretch in prison. For one thing they didn't let you drink there, and I couldn't possibly survive without drinking. It would be better if I were killed in the attempt.

I couldn't be sure I was only fantasizing because I could feel myself getting nuttier every day, more cornered and desperate. Something had to happen one way or another.

I continued to give readings with the group. The other guys could have had no idea what was going on with me. On the surface I think I acted carefree and cheerful – but that was my pride covering up. I pretended not to take writing too seriously. They only saw me when I was amply fuelled and able to roll. If I drank enough I almost appeared to be a normal human being. Sometimes I felt like one. You might have caught me onstage at Loyola boisterously singing a song I wrote, mixing the verses in with one of my new stories. Did I look like a guy with troubles? A real Maritimer, that fellow, give him a drink and watch him go. You can tell a guy who's enjoying life.

There was another frustrated literary giant in Montreal in those days, Bryan McCarthy, the poet. He was a gifted writer, but a trifle lazy I'm afraid – he didn't write much but had great expectations from what he did. He got the idea to form a performance group of his own: himself, me, and a broken-down alkie and former jazz musician named

Art Houston. Bryan was to read poetry, I'd do poems and stories, and Art would do a vaudeville comedy routine – "I stayed in a hotel once, the room was so small the bedbugs were hunchbacked!" Inspired stuff, bad enough that you had to chuckle despite yourself, at least I did. We were billed as The Rank Outsiders, and I have to say we were so much what we were called that despite Bryan's sending notices of our availability to all the schools in Montreal we got no offers. The only appearance we ever made was at the Boiler Room on Crescent Street as part of a larger performance – readings and recitations and songs by a collection of Montreal talents that included Willie Dunn, Ron Lee, Mario Gross, Manuel Santos-Betanzos, Graham McKeen, and the three aforementioned. I guess most of us were of the outsider variety and two-fisted boozers to boot. It was a pretty slapdash affair, followed by a spirited drunkfest, the beer being on the house for the entertainers. (Some scenes come back to me – Bryan looking like George Bernard Shaw striding up and down among the tables and screaming his poems above the disruptive chatter of some drunken patrons... Graham indifferent to modern verse giving a dramatic delivery of "The Shooting of Dan McGrew"... Willie Dunn strumming his guitar and singing his lonesome Indian songs, the highlight of the show... Ron Lee the Gypsy reciting a vicious poetic diatribe against the politicians of Montreal – "*Drapeau the fascist!*"...)

I knew The Rank Outsiders would amount to nothing, one of assorted wild schemes of Bryan's, but I went along with the idea to please him; he'd have done the same for me. The last I heard from him he was in England. He wrote to tell me, "I'm now a half-assed carpenter who keeps getting fired." This was after belonging to a primal scream commune in Ireland until they kicked him out. His primal scream must have been like nothing they'd heard before.

For reasons unfathomable by me, God who knows every hair on our heads has been in the habit of intervening in my extremes to keep me writing, and out of jail, the madhouse and the grave. I had made my yearly application to the Canada Council, but my hopes were of the slimmest kind, considering the way I saw my luck as running. But I was hanging in to find out, it was the last card being dealt in that particular hand. I hate to think what the next deal would have been had I not got the grant; but as it happened I did. There was no elation this time, only a grim consciousness that I'd had a narrow escape, miraculously saved at the last instant. A very sober reaction – rare for me. Being crazy, however, a mocking voice in my head kept saying, "Your cup runneth over, your cup runneth over." It wouldn't stop, going on maddeningly. "But it doesn't," I answered. "Stop saying that." I knew what I had now

was an opportunity, not a reward. I couldn't act frivolously with this money; in my condition I was convinced my life depended on putting every penny to work.

My first act was to call Kenneth Hertz and ask his advice on getting a book printed. I was aware that doing my own book would involve numerous problems, and lies, and probably humiliation – "So nobody else would touch it, eh? Had to put it out yourself. Ha Ha!" Like some old spinster and her religious verses blowing her savings at a vanity press.

I should say that after Doubleday I hadn't sent *The Black Horse Tavern* to another publisher because I felt it would be a waste of stamps. I was full-up with rejections, no room for any more. I had almost forgotten I'd given Hertz a copy of the manuscript one day when he dropped by. He had a small publishing outfit called Ingluvin, and some time after he told me he would like to do the book, but he didn't know when, he had other commitments, maybe someday... that sort of thing. It could take years if ever, and I had no patience; I'd never had any, but now especially I felt I couldn't wait much longer. Better to see to the job myself, then I could be sure it would get done.

When I called him he said, "I don't know why you want to publish it yourself. I said I'd do it."

"Yeah, but when?"

"Well, I'm almost finished with Pat Lowther's book. I can get to yours next."

He sounded as if he meant it. I wanted to believe him, because the way I am, once I consider doing something almost any alternative looks better. I project catastrophic outcomes. Here was an appealing option, the job taken out of my hands. I'd get my book done and have my money too. What more could I ask for?

"They're good stories," I said. "You won't be embarrassed."

"I know. I like them."

"You mean you read them?"

"Of course I read them!" He was properly indignant. "Do you think I'd publish something I hadn't read?"

"I suppose not."

It must sound strange, but I'd come to believe that what you wrote had nothing to do with a publisher's decision. I didn't know how you could influence those people, if they were people. Maybe they flipped coins or cut cards or threw darts at names on the wall. If it was the case – as some maintained – that you had to know one personally, then perhaps it followed that the content and quality of your work wasn't a factor.

Now that I could see some light I thought possibly I'd come around a hairpin bend and was on the way out of the noxious tunnel I'd been stumbling around in. But it was an elusive light, a false light actually; things didn't really get any better for the next ten years. The story of how *The Black Horse Tavern* got published would discourage I don't know how many would-be writers. But the book did finally come out, and I'm grateful to Kenneth Hertz. And two novels – one runner-up for the Governor General's Award, for what that's worth – and a biography followed, from three different publishers. Nothing went smoothly, and none of it was easy, often because of my obsessive and unrealistic expectations.

It so happens I'm sober – but not solemn, not sombre – nowadays, thanks where thanks belong, and it's been a rejuvenating experience in many ways. I'm writing at a fine clip and while some days are inevitably exasperating I'm generally enjoying it. I feel I'm in the neighbourhood of where I ought to have been all along, where it's the work itself that counts and not what might happen because of it. It's nice to knock off some words every day, do my bit.

As for the Story Tellers, I left Montreal and the group when I got the grant, and I don't know how they fared after, except of course they fell apart. But what could you have expected?

I wish them well, each and all of them. It was a privilege treading the boards in the company of such distinguished strolling players.[3]

Nice & Paris, 1983

AFTERWORD

Reading this memoir over today I can see I was making every effort to be rigorously honest about myself and charitable towards others – including, it should be said, John Metcalf, who had published some unflattering views about me around this time. I thought the portrait he drew quite picturesque, and however askew at least expressed his interpretation of events. I can't pretend I always made a good impression in my drunken days.

John is a personable person in person, but in print he can be somewhat on the malignant side. If I may reciprocate with a slight analysis of my own, I'd say his main character flaw is envying the success and talent of others. It shows, for example, in his attacks on successful writers like Margaret Atwood, and on talented writers like myself. It's a common failing with ambitious people, and really a terrible way to have to live.

Which is not to say he's just some sort of shrewish literary gossip columnist. He's also a very good public reader who knows how to make his lines sound funny. As a performer he reminds me of the gifted British actor Rowan Atkinson of "Black Adder" and "Mr Bean" fame.

But Mr Bean isn't his chief inspiration. His writing – indeed his whole literary persona – is patterned after his idol, Kingsley Amis. If you like "Lucky Jim", as I do, you can't help but enjoy some of John's narratives. There's probably no one better at doing the Amis style of acid indignation. He's also a big fan of P.G. Wodehouse and I believe considers him to be a first-rate writer.

But enough of literary criticism. I hope the above has served to relieve some of John's guilt for the scurvy feelings he's had about me. I'll just add that contrary to his (and indeed my own) disparaging assessment of my skills as a public reader, I was never really that bad, and have become over the years one of the finest in the country, and if you don't believe me I'll gladly prove it for a suitable fee.

Fredericton, 2007

(This is the cowboy tale I read while with the Montreal Story Tellers. As a boy I took in hundreds of westerns at the old Capitol and Vogue theatres in Chatham, and in my mid-teens went through a period where I read about a 100 cowboy novels from my father's collection of pocketbooks. With all that lore in my head it would have been a shame not to write at least one such story myself.)

THE LARSEN BOYS

My name is Dan Forest and I'm an old man now and not much good for anything but telling stories, not that there's anything wrong with that. Someone has to pass on what life was like in Pittsfield's bygone days, otherwise the people from back then will be forgotten forever, like they never lived at all.

I'm thinking of incidents like this one from my childhood, the highlight of which I myself witnessed from the roof of O'Leary's stables, across from Duffy's Saloon. The reason for it all, what happened behind the scenes you might say, I only learned later that summer by hanging about the front veranda of the Touraine Hotel, where most of the old gaffers hung out (old gaffers such as I am myself now!). These wizened-up left-over specimens of humanity were as much a fixture in the heart of town as the gallows beside the sheriff's office, and like all such codgers, they loved to tip back their chairs and spit tobacco and blather and yarn by the hour. I don't believe they ever noticed me sitting quietly on the steps. I was just a kid at the time and nobody paid attention to kids in those days. But I was listening – I always had my ears wide open. I was ever the curious type.

People today might find my style a bit on the dramatic side, but it's the way stories were told in olden times, and it's too late for me to change my ways now. If you don't like it you can ask for your money back.

❖

As I heard it, Bass Robichaud took the news without hardly a change in expression, except for his eyes, they turned hard and cold. He gazed a minute or two down Water Street, then went into the feed store he owned and strapped on his gun. When he came out he said, "Tell folks to keep their heads down. There's going to be lead flying mighty soon."

Word was soon all over town, all the citizens tearing around and button-holing their neighbours. "The women and children!" they said to each other. "What about our families?"

"We got to do something."

"What can we do?"

"I say we hold a meeting!"

"Good idea! Spread it around. We'll meet in Duffy's Saloon."

In the saloon the men ordered up and talked among themselves in worried tones, until Mayor Tom Cribbs took the floor.

"Quiet, everyone! Quiet! Let's have some order here!"

The conversations died down, then ceased altogether.

"Now," said Tom Cribbs, "is everyone on hand?"

A pause. Someone shouted, "Judge Bushy, he ain't here yet!'

"That's right," another voice cried. "Where's the Judge?"

"Someone go fetch him," said the Mayor. "We'll hold things up till he gets here."

At this moment Judge Bushy was inside Bass Robichaud's feed store talking with Bass. He had rushed over as soon as he heard the news.

The Judge was an elderly man with a mass of white hair, and his face wore a grave expression.

"Bass," he said, "I understand how you feel, but it might be best if you left town. There's three of them, you know. And Sheriff O'Toole won't be any help. He's laid up sick with the pox and is in no shape to face any kind of gunslinger, let alone the Larsen brothers. I tell you that man shouldn't have the job anyway. If he weren't the Mayor's brother-in-law he'd be back sweeping floors in Polly's whorehouse where he belongs."

"Now hold 'er right there, Judge. You mean to say you want me to saddle up and ride out?"

"It's an old man's advice, Bass. We both know what the Larsens are like. They're bad cusses. I'd rather face a bear with a burr up his arse."

Bass looked straight into the Judge's eyes.

"I thought you knowed me better than that, Judge," he said. "I can't run away from these outlaws. This is my home – I was born and raised here. If I run away now I'll be running all my life."

The Judge sighed. "I was afraid you'd say that, Bass. And I guess I'd have said the same in your place." He paused. His mouth tightened. "Well, I'm not letting you face them skunks alone. Give me a gun!"

Bass put a restraining hand on the Judge's arm. "No. This ain't your fight, Judge. I have to do this by myself."

Judge Bushy protested.

"No," repeated Bass. "For my sake stay out of it. I don't want to see none of my friends get hurt."

"I don't care, Bass," said the Judge. "This is one time you need a friend. When the shooting starts you can bet your life I'll be right there beside you."

Judge Bushy left the store.

Well, thought Bass, I tried. But it was comforting to know he'd have one man at least to back him up. It was no easy chore facing three killers alone.

The Judge had started up the street when Augustine Smith, the tailor, intercepted him and told him about the citizen's meeting. Judge Bushy followed him to Duffy's Saloon.

Back in the feed store Bass Robichaud pulled out his Colt and rolled the chamber, checking that all six cylinders were filled. He hadn't fired it since he was Marshall in Newton, but he'd made a point to keep it well oiled. In the back of his mind he'd always known this day would come.

"Six shells, three Larsens," he muttered.

He put an extra handful of cartridges into his pocket and went to the window.

At that moment the door burst open. Bass turned like a cat, hand flying lightning-quick to his holster.

"Bass!" It was Millie Malley, Bass's fiancée, who owned the little milliner's shop on Duke Street. "Bass, I just heard. Oh!" She was sobbing. Bass caught her in his arms, held her to his chest.

"Oh, Bass," she sobbed, "what will you do?"

"Face them, I guess. There's nothing else I can do."

"Oh, you can't, Bass. They'll kill you. Think who they are – you know how much they hate you for sending them to the penitentiary."

Bass said nothing.

"I love you, Bass," said Millie, her voice trembling. "I love you. For my sake get away from here. Take me with you. We can get married in Richibucto or somewhere and keep moving. We'll settle in a place where they won't find us."

"I can't, Millie. You got to understand that."

She began sobbing again. "How can I understand it? I love you. I don't want to see you killed. Please, Bass."

Bass patted her shoulder. In his eyes there was a faraway look.

"I can't run away, Millie. If I run away I'll be running all my life. Please don't ask me no more."

"Oh, Bass!" she cried, holding him tight.

A man appeared in the doorway.

"Bass, we just held a citizens' meeting in the saloon," he said. "We'd like you to mosey on over."

Bass broke himself away from Millie and followed the man. As they walked across the dusty street Millie leaned her cheek against the doorframe, tears coming from her eyes.

It was a short walk to Duffy's Saloon, their footsteps echoing sharply on the board sidewalk. It was cooler in the saloon and fairly dark at first, after the bright mid-day sun. Bass stepped inside the door and stopped there, eyeing the seated men.

Mayor Tom Cribbs got to his feet and cleared his throat.

"Well, Bass," said the Mayor, "we just held a meeting, as citizens of this town, and what we discussed – well, you probably figured it out already. It's the Larsen boys. We all know they're coming to town to get you, and the menfolks around here is worried. Now don't get us wrong – it ain't ourselves we're worried about, it's the woman and children. If it was just us we'd be behind you all the way. But we got families. If you get one of them galoots afore the others get you there'll be the devil to pay. Them boys can get mighty riled up. Women and children mean nothing to varmints like them. They'll plunder and rape and burn and kill and God knows what kinda hell and tarnation they'll leave behind."

"You tell him, Tommy!"

"Be jaysus! And me after puttin' new windas in me store!"

"Yeah! Them boys kin shoot!" Suddenly voices were raised everywhere.

"That Buck Larsen, he could shoot the balls off a gopher at a hundred yard."

"Buck's nothin' compared to Bart. Why, Bart could shoot the balls off a termite at a thousand yard."

"I guess you ain't never seen Bat. Bat's the one, boys. He's yer man! That son of a horse thief! He could shoot the eyes out of a potato that ain't been dug yet. I seen him do it. From two mile away! And atween his legs, too. With a blindfold on – "

"Guns is nothin'! Dagnabit! The way them boys handle a knife – they could have your hide off and sold at auction afore you started shakin' from the cold!"

"Okay, lads, that's enough. Hold it now! Will yez all shut up!" Mayor Cribbs hollered till he had their attention. "I know how yez feel. Being the banker in this town I probably got the most to lose of anyone. But don't forget, that ain't the point. We're trying to protect the women and children. Now, Bass, we know the only reason the Larsens is coming to town is to get you. If you wasn't here they'd be content to stay home in Skunk Ridge where they belong. After five years in the pen, why, they'd be laying around with their old granny drinking that fine moonshine they make – resting up, like. And then after a spell, when they was good and ready, they could light out to track you down. But they wouldn't come here, see? if you was some place else. And they might be years catching you. You understand that? So what we done, we took a vote and decided it'd be best for everyone concerned if you saddled up and got outa town. And the faster the better." He gestured to a wad of bills on the table at his side. "See that there money? We ain't hard-hearted, Bass. Some of us pooled together and come up with enough to buy your store. It ain't a bad price, today's market being what it is and this a quick sale and all. I'm sorry, Bass, we all like you very much, but we got our families to think of. We knew you'd understand. So would you take the money and – "

"I don't need the money."

"What? But Bass! Take a little of it, anyway. You'll need a grubstake for the trail —"

"I don't need the money cuz I ain't leaving town."

A mumbling and growling went up from the men. Bass raised his voice and they fell quiet.

"I know you mean well, but when the Larsens ride in I'll be here waiting for 'em. And I'll tell you why. If I left town I'd be doing just what the Larsen boys and all the outlaws like them want me to do. There's a greater thing at stake here than my life... greater than the lives of your families, even. I mean justice, decency, the right for people to live good honest lives. You see, I thought this out. I figured someday them sidewinders would be coming for me. When I put them behind bars they said they'd get me. You all know that. But I decided I couldn't run away. It wouldn't be right. Apart from the fact that if I started running I'd be running all my life, there was something more important at stake here. It's our whole way of life. If we let ourselves be scared by outlaws then this ain't a land of freedom and justice, but a dunghill of crime and a vale of tears. If we believe in the things we stand for then we got to be ready to stand up and fight for them."

The saloon was silent.

"So are you with me?"

In the stillness he could hear the grandfather clock ticking. A fly buzzed over a drop of spilt rotgut. A splat of chewing tobacco hit the floor.

Bass Robichaud ran his eyes over the crowd.

"Where's Judge Bushy?" he said.

"He was here a minute ago, over by the bar. He must've left."

Bass nodded. "I reckon there's someone asides myself figures it's time to quit palaverin' and tie on a shootin' iron."

Ignoring the outburst of guffaws, Bass said, "I put them hooty owls away once. This time I intend to finish the job."

A voice hollered from the bar, "Yeah, but back then they was dead drunk. And ya had five deputies with ya!"

"It don't make no difference. When a man's got right on his side he's got all the deputies he needs."

Bass Robichaud turned on his heel and left.

As he walked across to his store he heard behind him the sound of an earnest discussion breaking out in the saloon.

❖

The afternoon moved on and the shadows grew longer. Pittsfield was like a ghost town, the streets deathly quiet, deserted. Dust swirled in a gust of wind and settled. Behind locked doors and shuttered windows the townfolk waited anxiously for the eruption of gunfire and bloodshed.

A boy galloped frantically into town, his horse panting and in a lather. He pulled up before Bass Robichaud's feed store.

"They're coming!" he shouted. "The Larsens! They're ridin' into town!"

He galloped away, leaving the streets empty once again.

Bass Robichaud stepped out of his store. With his gun slung low he waited a long minute, standing alone, gazing in the direction the Larsen's would come from.

Somewhere in the distance a coyote howled.

A clump of sagebrush blew past and caught against the hitching post outside O'Leary's stables.

He pulled the brim of his stetson down.

He saw them as they rounded the corner of Cunard Street, three horsemen riding slowly along Water Street towards him. The Larsen boys. He took a deep breath. He could hear the muted thud of horse hoofs in the dust, drawing closer. Thoughts raced through his mind. *Bart kin shoot the balls off a termite at a thousand yard!... I guess you ain't never seen Bat. Bat's the one, boy. He's yer man! He kin shoot the eye out of a potato from two mile away...* Bass tried to swallow but his mouth was dry as powder. He was aware of a nervous tremor in his bowels. They were still a long ways off but he couldn't afford to wait any longer. He yelled, "Look behind you, boys!" then went for his gun and fired. The three horsemen continued to ride towards him at the same gait. He wiped the sweat out of his eyes with his sleeve. Dropping to one knee he aimed along the barrel of his gun. His right hand was shaking. Steadying the gun with both hands he fired and missed. He fired again, but it was still long range and his shot went wide, kicking up a tuft of dirt beyond the Larsens. In desperation he dropped to his belly. With his elbows resting on the ground he drew aim again. They were closer now, he could see the tails of their long beige coats flapping in the breeze. He squeezed the trigger. Another miss. He had only two rounds left in the chamber. Scrambling to his feet he dashed toward a water trough for cover.

It was close. He dove just as the Larsen boys slapped leather and shots rang out. His body twisted in the air and he fell on his back in the dirt. Three holes in the water trough sent three thin streams of water splashing down on him. Half his head was blown away.

As he lay on the ground his sightless eyes stared up at a young boy peering over the edge of the roof of O'Leary's stables.

A woman screamed. It was Millie. She was crouched behind a window in her milliner's shop, not far from where Bass had fallen. She started to get up and run out to him but something held her back. The Larsens were coming nearer.

Crouching down again she prayed they didn't know where the scream had come from.

When the Larsens were upon Bass they fired several shots into his dead body. Bart Larsen rode over him with his horse, then the three wheeled about and headed out of town, talking amongst themselves.

Old Jim McInnerny, who'd taken cover in an empty molasses puncheon outside the general store, overheard them as they trotted by.

"Boys, that was nice shootin' I done back there."

"Yep! I reckon I took care of that hombre once and for all."

"Now hold on there, Bat. You ain't sayin' you dropped that dude."

"He's a lowdown liar, Buck. There ain't but one man coulda kilt that galoot with him a-flyin' through the air like that, and I ain't afeared to say it was me."

"Why, you weasel-faced horntoad. That tin-horn was half-fried in Hell afore you'd even cleared leather. You hear me, Bart?"

"I tell ya, my hogleg was a-spittin' lead afore..."

Meanwhile, back in the saloon Mayor Tom Cribbs turned away

from the open window he'd been looking out and said, "See, they're gone. I told you'd they'd leave soon as Bass was dead."

"That was smart thinking, Mayor," said alderman Zeke Harding, taking the smoking shotgun from him.

Everybody was breathing easier. They congratulated the Mayor.

"Drinks are on the house!" cried Big Bill Duffy, the saloon owner.

They were all talking and laughing at once, overcome with relief.

"Now the women and children are safe!'

"Bass shoulda listened to reason."

"Stubborn as a mule. It's what comes of readin' all them dime novels. Puts a lot of foolish ideas in a man's head."

"Well, they ain't in his head now. There ain't *nothin'* in his head. Har! Har!"

"Let's drink to the Mayor!"

"Where's the Judge?"

"Anyone seen the Judge?"

Up in his room Judge Bushy shook the last drop out of a whisky bottle and tossed it in the corner. His window was shut and the blind pulled down. A chest of drawers barricaded the door.

"Them Larsen skunks... Oughta be hung, all of 'em. Give 'em the rope they ever come before me... hang the lot of 'em!" Glossy-eyed, he looked cautiously at the door. He was getting old, talking aloud to himself like that. No telling where them varmints were. Now where'd he put that other bottle?

Down in the street Millie took one look at Bass Robichaud's face and threw up into the water trough.

MASKS

One night when I was twelve, back in the fifties, Arnie Flynn and I slept out in a clubhouse that four of us guys had made from an old hen house. The place still smelled like a hen house, but nothing to what it had been when we started, when there was straw, feathers and chicken shit a foot deep on the floor, and a good deal of the last-mentioned spattered all over the walls. It took us a month of shovelling and sweeping and scrubbing and whitewashing to whip the place into shape. Another of our friends, Buck Connors, had talked his father into letting us have it, since the Connors's hadn't kept chickens for years, and the shack was just sitting at the back of their yard and rotting away.

We built two sets of double bunks, one on each side of the room, out of some weather-beaten lumber we rounded up from here and there, and we covered the walls with cardboard and the cardboard with baseball and hockey cards and pictures of pirate ships and jet planes and racing cars and the like, things we cut out of magazines. We made a table out of orange crates for playing checkers and cards and monopoly on, and we found some log stumps to use for chairs. For a while we had a calendar with a photo of a pretty girl in an Esther Williams one-piece bathing suit on the wall, but Buck's father saw it and gave us hell for having indecent pictures and made us to take it down.

It was to be our first night sleeping in our new clubhouse. There should have been four of us, but Buck came down with a bad cold at the last minute, and the mother of our other friend, Jack Landon, was keeping him in that weekend after catching him smoking.

Although it was still early September, my Uncle Gerald had just given me a rubber Halloween mask he'd come across in his attic, which was probably the ugliest and most frightening mask I'd ever seen. It was an old witch's face with a pointy chin and a toothless grinning mouth and a large nose with a black wart on the end of it.

When I saw it I thought of a comic book I'd run across a few years earlier, before grisly crime and horror and sexually suggestive comics were banned by the government to protect young kids like myself. One of the stories in it was about a man who met the young lady of his dreams (so he thought) at a New Year's Eve costume party. She was dressed as a harem girl in a skimpy costume like a belly dancer's, and she had an excitingly beautiful figure. Even though her face was hidden behind an ugly witch mask it was easy to see why she'd caught the man's eye.

He introduced himself, and soon they were dancing the night away. They danced and drank champagne and got along wonderfully, and when the clock struck midnight and he took his mask off to embrace her, to his surprise she insisted on keeping hers on. And when he took her home and they were getting ready for bed she still wouldn't take off her mask.

She said it was a New Year's custom in the old country where her parents came from, and he'd just have to put up with it, and if he didn't like it he could always leave.

The man was dying to know what she looked like, but he didn't want to go home, and so decided to humour her. But in the night he awoke and seeing the moonlight shining on her sleeping form, was unable to resist satisfying his curiosity.

He just knew she was going to be gorgeous. Her voice, her laugh, her body, everything led him to expect it.

Very gently he untied and lifted the mask, and drew back with a gasp. For a moment he thought he was seeing things. Gazing up at him from the pillow was the same face he'd just removed! A horribly ugly old hag's face with a pointy chin and a toothless mouth and a large nose with a black wart on the end of it. The man's cry woke the girl. Then all at once he started laughing. "Oh, I get it! You're wearing a second mask! Ha ha! You were afraid of the first one falling off. Let me take this one off too!"

"No!" the girl cried.

"But I have to see what you look like. I know you're going to be absolutely beautiful."

And he tugged at the mask, and tugged, and tugged, and the girl screamed, but he wouldn't stop until he'd ripped it away. Then he sank back, and with it hanging from his hands, dripping, he saw what she'd been afraid of. Staring up at him was a bloody mush where her face had been. It hadn't been a mask at all but her real face. *He had pulled the skin clean off her skull...*

It was a gruesome story, with scenes an impressionable mind like mine wasn't likely to forget.

And now I had become owner of that very face, or at any rate a mask that looked exactly like it (not that I could imagine the body that went with it ever being young and shapely). And what was I thinking of doing with it? I thought I'd bring it with me when Arnie and I slept out.

As I told Jack Landon on our way home from school, my plan was put it on in the middle of the night and sneak over to Arnie's bunk and shine a penlight under my chin and tap him awake and scare the living daylights out of him.

It was dark when we lugged our bedding to the clubhouse, and I had no trouble sneaking the mask and a penlight in and slipping them under my pillow. We lit our kerosene lamp and got the cards out and played Auction Forty-five for an hour or so, and then blew the lamp out and climbed into our bunks. Arnie's was the lower bunk on one side of the room and mine was the upper on the other. For a time we lay talking, passing the odd comment back and forth, until at length there was silence, not a sound except for the wind shaking the trees outside. It was a cloudy night and pitch dark in the room.

As I lay there I could hear the wind rise and fall, at times almost shrieking, then dropping to a moan. Sometimes it would stop altogether, and it was very quiet then – as quiet as the grave, as the saying goes. I thought about my rubber mask, but the joke, for some reason, had become not as interesting as in the afternoon. Perhaps it was the darkness, which seemed darker than other nights. Perhaps it was the wind, or the thought of that old crone's evil wrinkled features. Seeing her in my mind in her black rags, her body grown aged and bent and twisted, wandering the night in search of her face. Crouching somewhere, waiting to spring up with her bony hands and razor-sharp fingernails...

In a strange place in the pitch dark with the wind howling and the walls creaking it was easy to have such thoughts.

So as I lay in my bunk, instead of preparing to scare Arnie, I found that I was growing more than a little on the scared side myself. My eyes were wide open, my ears attuned for any sound, all my senses straining. The strangest notions ran through my mind. What, I asked myself, do I *really* know about Arnie? What does anyone *really* know about anyone else, other than what they let you see?

I remembered Clarence Haley, one of the town drunks, who'd been found dead that summer behind the graveyard, his head smashed in. Nobody ever found out who did it. Where, I wondered, was Arnie that August night? At home? With his family his alibi? I thought of his family – but there it was. What did I know about his father and mother, brothers and sisters? It struck me that, after all, they were strangers, hidden most of the time behind the walls of their house. Only they themselves knew what went on behind those walls. They could be a family of ghouls or devil worshippers or homicidal maniacs, for all I could tell. I considered them in my mind, went over the family one by one, and to my horror realized that each of them *could* be what I feared.

What if Arnie had just been waiting for a night like this to get me alone?

I listened for his breathing, trying to detect if he was asleep or only pretending. Thinking his voice might give him away, I gathered my courage and asked as calmly as I could if he was still awake. He didn't answer. I asked again, louder. His breathing checked. "What?"

"Nothing. I thought you might be awake. I don't feel very sleepy."

He dozed off again, or apparently did. I knew he would wait until later before coming for me. He might even be cold-blooded enough to actually sleep until an hour before dawn, and then slip stealthily out of bed and tiptoe across the room and use the butcher knife he'd sneaked into the clubhouse and hidden under his pillow, as I'd done with my mask...

I thought of my mask and the cruel irony of it. My great practical joke! I could no more get up now and go over to that bunk...

I tried again to shake off my fears, telling myself I was letting my imagination run away with me. If I kept on like this, cowering in my bunk, what was I to tell Jack Landon in the morning? We'd had such a laugh picturing the scare I'd give Arnie. How was I to explain not going through with it?

But I couldn't convince myself. Best friend or not, I was by now thoroughly persuaded that the boy in the bunk across the room was planning to kill me. And I couldn't do anything about it for fear of being mistaken, other than resolve to fight to the last gasp when the moment came.

I expected to stay awake all night, but exhaustion got the better of me, for I did drop off, eventually. It was a fitful sleep, and I woke several times breathless with fear, staring into the dark, heart pounding, not daring to move. I listened for the sound of bare feet on the floor, thinking that was what had awakened me, that I'd heard him approaching in my sleep. And now he was standing near me, behind my head. And I was afraid to turn and look for fear he'd strike.

The last time I awoke it was daylight, some minutes after seven. The reality of morning poured through the window and I was still alive, and Arnie was in his little bunk across the floor, still lost to the world.

Of course I felt relieved. But I was also chagrined and disgusted with myself, as I thought of my mask and the joke I hadn't pulled. In a last face-saving effort I crawled from my bunk and went over and tapped Arnie on the shoulder. I had my mask on, and he opened his eyes and looked at me. He grinned, gave a little chuckle, stretched and went back to sleep.

One way and another, by means of subject-changing and half-statements, I hummed and hawed my way through the account I owed Jack Landon of the affair, and since Arnie was nowhere around, simulated the shocked look on his face at the sight of the mask staring down at him *in the middle of the night.* But my heart wasn't in it, and I dwelt as briefly as possible on the story, though Jack wanted to hear it in detail.

HOOFBEATS IN THE NIGHT

My memories of Christmas as a young lad in Chatham flood back on me as I hear the words of that old Christmas chestnut running through my head:

Chestnuts roasting on an open fire...

Even though we didn't have an open fire in our house (other than when we took the lid off the woodstove to thrown another stick in), and consequently no place to roast the chestnuts, it didn't really matter, since we had no chestnuts either. The first (and only and last) chestnut I ever ate was from a street vendor in Seville many years later when I was grown up, and it was nothing like the song had led me to expect, being dry, mushy and more or less tasteless. So we didn't really miss anything.

And then there was the turkey and some mistletoe.

Everybody knows a turkey and some mistletoe...

We were only a small family of five so our turkeys weren't ever full-grown ones, having been killed while still at the chicken stage. The way we looked at it (or I presume we did), it was like lamb versus mutton or veal versus cow – the younger and smaller was better than the older and bigger. We never complained, I know that much. Chicken was plenty feast enough for us in those hard-up times – definitely a step up from salt cod, baloney and beans.

I don't recollect a lot of mistletoe hanging about. I believe I was twenty-three when I first set eyes on any. I was told by a young lady it was a tradition to stand beneath it, after she'd been standing beneath it for a while giving me peculiar looks. I didn't ask her why, not wanting to seem stupid, but when she left the room I thought I'd try it myself. But nothing happened to me either.

The part of the song I'm edging up to is the tiny tots with their eyes all aglow, who'll find it hard to sleep tonight. That was me to the core. And the line about

> *every mother's child is going to spy*
> *to see if reindeer really know how to fly...*

I did that, slipped from my bed and peeped out the window at the starry sky to see if I could spot Santa's sleigh sailing overhead, coming in for a landing on our roof. Every Christmas I took a peek, but never made a single sighting.

And then, at the age of something or other, an amazing thing happened. I was tossing in bed with my eyes all aglow when thump! thump! thump! I heard reindeer on the rooftop. Dancer, Prancer, Cupid, Vixen, Dasher, Donder, Comet and Blitzen... stomping and champing and jingling their bells while the jolly old fellow with his bulging belly like a bowl full of jelly set about climbing down our chimney.

I raced to the window and peered through the frosted panes, but naturally I couldn't see anything, with the sleigh being up on the rooftop. But I *heard*. I heard a bunch of *ho ho hoes!* that thrilled me to the marrow. I was about to dash downstairs to see Santa climb out of our stove – we didn't have a fireplace – but my mother intercepted me.

It wasn't the thing to do, catching Santa in the act, she said (which I already knew, but hadn't been able to contain myself). She said that by now old St Nick would be in the kitchen having the tea and fruit cake we'd left out, and it would be impolite to interrupt him. Not to mention good little boys were supposed to be asleep in their beds at this hour. If Santa knew I was up chances were he wouldn't leave me anything; I'd be lucky to get the dreaded potato at the bottom of my sock. So I stayed in bed.

I don't recall it bothering my mind how a large-waisted man like Santa Claus ever made it through the pipe connecting the chimney to our stove. Or how he navigated the stove itself. But then, I had no problem with how he got to the chimney in the first place, soaring through the air on a sleigh. It was just one of those things he did.

It was still dark when my father got up and lit the oil lamps (we had no electricity in those days) and stoves. I had to wait through that, too, for the downstairs to warm up. Twisting and turning, clawing the air, practically jumping out of my skin.

Finally my mother gave me the go ahead sign. Like a coiled spring I shot from my bed and flew down the stairs. First stop was my stocking hanging on the wall in the kitchen (actually one of my sisters' long cotton stockings, since my own knitted wool socks wouldn't have held enough). I squeezed out the contents: an apple, an orange, some unshelled nuts, licorice, bubblegum, a handful of striped Christmas candies. Any other time of the year this would have been a wealth of unaccustomed treats, but today it was just for starters. Tossing my horde aside I made a beeline for the front room where our tree was set up.

We had a small wood stove in the front room, and it was blazing away, happy to be of service. It was the only time we ever lit this stove, Christmas – indeed, it was almost the only time of year the room itself was ever used. It was our best room, and was kept ready for some special occasion in the future, which I don't believe ever came. It would have taken a visit from King George VI to open it up, I think.

Although, come to think of it, my oldest sister Carmel did entertain her boyfriend and future husband John there. He was an RCAF pilot who I eventually found out wasn't coming to see me in order to tell me all about flying planes, but (which was all right too) to give me a dime to make myself scarce.

Over the years there were many gifts from Santa under the tree, going way back to things like a wooden rocking horse and picture books and colouring books and crayons and coloured putty and a magic slate. And one year a sled with red runners, and another a brown cart, and every year games like snakes & ladders, checkers, Chinese checkers, crokinole. And a card game called Authors with pictures of Charles Dickens, Samuel Taylor Coleridge, Sir Walter Scott and Mark Twain. And a box of little metal cowboys and Indians with their weapons held in various fighting poses. And a small wind-up train on an oval track. And a "leopard-skin" cloth cowboy vest and chaps and a pair of spurs and a cap-gun six-shooter with holster and belt. And two books.

Not surprisingly, considering the course my life was to take, it's the books that left the deepest impression. I got them both the same year, when I was ten. I can't tell you the title of the first one, which was a collection of essays, stories and sections from novels by different writers; but I well remember the cover; it showed a rakish-looking buccaneer leaning on the rail of a sailing ship. They were magical tales, mostly of manly adventure, but some of romance, including a part from

Dickens's *Great Expectations* where the bewitching young girl tells Pip he may kiss her. When I read it that Christmas it had such power it took my breath away, almost threw me into a swoon. Never before and not since has a piece of writing had so strong an effect on me.

The other book was an adventure novel called *The Mercer Boys And The Cruise Of The Lassie*. It was of a different kind, strictly a boys' book, but it gave me enormous pleasure too, in its own way.

These were the first books I could call my own, and in themselves they were gifts, just by being books. I loved the look and smell and feel of them. By then I was already developing a chronic addiction to reading. I was like a dry and healthy alcoholic with a unopened bottle in his hands. It was great to admire the shape of the bottle, the label, the colour of the liquid, but the real joy was in the promise. The anticipation of uncapping it, savouring it, losing oneself in a warmth of euphoria... a delicious flight from reality.

Somewhat like Santa Claus and the Christmas experience, come to think of it.

The Cruise On The Lassie didn't let me down. It was a tale filled with adventure and mystery. A sailboat, an island, buried loot, villains to be thwarted. I can see *that* cover vividly as well, a shiny hard-cover with a life-like portrait of two older teenage boys on a sloop as it leaned into the wind, whitecaps on the water and sail billowing, one brother at the tiller and the other studying the sky for an approaching storm.

My parents and myself and my two sisters lived in one half of an old house in those days, sharing it with the Keatings, a family of ten kids (the ideal number for a family, to my envious mind). Being a little fellow I thought our dwelling places were of a fine and normal size, but in fact each had only a kitchen and a front room downstairs and three small rooms under the sloping roof upstairs. The basement was a dank cellar dug out of the earth down below, and there was no plumbing, and nothing like a bathroom, just a couple of outhouses, ours in our woodshed, theirs a stand-alone in the backyard.

Of course, the rent was only five dollars a month, so we couldn't expect to have everything.

On that one particular Christmas Eve – as I discovered later – a couple of the older Keating boys went up on the roof and tramped their feet and jingled some horse bells and ho-hoed for the benefit of the gullible younger set, which being under the same roof included myself.

I thought I ought to mention that before closing. I wouldn't want anyone going away thinking I still believe it was Santa and his reindeer up there.

MY TEN FAVOURITE BOOKS

Being one of the more prominent writers at my address on Shore Street, I get asked by admirers to do things like NAME MY TEN FAVOURITE BOOKS. This has happened at least once in the past thirty years, and since it would be convenient to have a list handy for the next occasion, I hereby and without further introduction present MY TEN FAVOURITE BOOKS in the order in which they come to mind. Although I first want to say ten was a big number, and I wasn't sure I could come up with that many. But there are definitely books I really liked at the time I read them, even if I've possibly outgrown some (not Stevenson and Carroll as you might think, but possibly one or two others).

Crime and Punishment, The Possessed, Notes From Underground and other novels – Fyodor Dostoievsky.
Great Expectations, Oliver Twist and *David Copperfield* – Charles Dickens.
Don Quixote – Miguel de Cervantes.
Huckleberry Finn, Innocents Abroad, Life on the Mississippi and *Roughing It* – Mark Twain.
Collected short stories and plays – Anton Tchekov.
Leaves of Grass – Walt Whitman.
Hamlet, MacBeth and the historical plays – William Shakespeare.
Alice in Wonderland & Through the Looking Glass – Lewis Carroll.
Gulliver's Travels – Jonathan Swift
Dubliners – James Joyce.
The Three Musketeers – Alexandre Dumas.

Journey to the End of Night and *Death on the Instalment Plan*
– Ferdinand de Celine.
Tom Jones – Henry Fielding.
Goodbye Mr Chips and *Lost Horizon* – James Hilton.
Tortilla Flat and *Cannery Row* – John Steinbeck.
For Whom the Bell Tolls and short stories – Ernest Hemingway.
Confessions – Jean-Jacques Rousseau.
Kidnapped and *Treasure Island* – Robert Louis Stevenson.
Dead Souls – Nickolai Gogol.
Typee – Herman Melville.
The Bounty Trilogy – Charles Nordhoff & James Hall
All Quiet on the Western Front, The Road Back and *Three Comrades*
– Erich Maria Remarque.
Tobacco Road – Erskine Caldwell.
Sons and Lovers – D. H. Lawrence.
The Way of All Flesh – Samuel Butler
Of Human Bondage – Somerset Maugham.
Martin Eden – Jack London.
Dracula – Bram Stoker.
Borstal Boy – Brendan Behan.
Tropic of Cancer – Henry Miller.
Down and Out in London and Paris – George Orwell.
Tristram Shandy – Lawrence Stern.
Wuthering Heights – Emily Bronte.
The Beautiful and the Damned – F. Scott Fitzgerald.
The Collected Stories – Damon Runyon.
Kenilworth (and other novels) – Walter Scott.
Lolita – Vladimir Nabokov

On the Yard – Malcolm Braly.
Cancer Ward and *The Gulag Archipelago* – Aleksandr Solzhenitsyn.
Pride and Prejudice – Jane Austin.
To Kill A Mockingbird – Harper Lee.
The Catcher In The Rye – J.D. Salinger.
On The Road – Jack Kerouac
The Complete Sherlock Holmes (novels & stories) – Arthur Conan Doyle.
The Boat Who Wouldn't Float and *Never Cry Wolf* – Farley Mowat.
Cabbagetown – Hugh Garner.
You May Know Them As Sea Urchins, Ma'am and *That Far Greater Bay* – Ray Guy.
St Urbain's Horseman – Mordecai Richler.
Cabbagetown Diary – Juan Butler.

The Wanton Troopers – Alden Nowlan.
Memoirs of Montparnasse – John Glassco.

There are many more I could name, including various memoirs, biographies and travel books, and quite a list of Canadian poets who flourished mostly in the 1960s and 70s; but I wanted to keep the number down around ten. For those who are curious to know *why* I liked the above books, the answer is simple: I liked them because I liked them. And if you've read them yourself and disagree with me it's probably because you *didn't* like them. And if you didn't like them the reason is because you have no taste.

WHY I SIT ON A BOARD

Since you ask, being on a Board of Directors is nothing new to me. For a couple of years I was on the Board of Directors of the Wild East Publishing Cooperative, and in the seventies I was Chairman of the Board of the Flat Earth Society. So I know most of what there is to know about Boards of Directors.

The main thing about the job is that it comes with a fine-sounding title. You can get cards printed up and hand them around wherever you go and right away people will take you for a person of quality and substance in the world – you can fool them that way.

Other than that, a Board of Directors is a group of individuals who get together periodically for a meeting and then return to where they came from.

As the result of a thorough study of humility, my enthusiasm for status and prestige (as I was telling King James over coffee at his Palace just last week) has left me entirely; and – as everyone knows – meetings of a Board (of any kind) have been known to leave a body bored (hence the saying, stiff as a board)... so why did I accept the position? That is the question.

Some other questions are: Who am I? Why do I exist?

I have a c/v in front of me and I'll check it to see if it has the answers.

All I really want to say is I was born in Chatham, NB, and now live in Fredericton. And that I'm here on Earth for a good reason, even if I don't know what it is. I agreed to accept a position on the Writer's Federation of New Brunswick Board of Directors because someone asked me to, and if I'm asked to do something I like to accommodate (unless I can come up with a good excuse and get out of it which I couldn't that day).

As for the rest, here it is. Age: middling, but can be mistaken for younger at times, like ten or eleven. Marital status: eligible bachelor (divorced), kind, considerate, likes good music, travel, walks in the moonlight, sex. Please send photo.

Besides various parts of New Brunswick I've lived in Montreal, Toronto, Ireland, Spain and France.

I've been writing for a good many years. I don't want to go around bragging about all the awards I've won, because I would only be lying, not having won any. I did make it to runner-up for the Governor General's Award once, behind what's-her-name, Alice Munro, but it's true what they say in sporting circles – nobody remembers who comes second.

I was told to keep this to 250-350 words and I've run over which means it's time to slap down the old *-30-* (a little touch that suggests I was also a journalist at one time).

– 30 –

REX

To this day barking dogs get on my nerves. It's true a lot of other noises do too, and noise pollution *is* a genuine problem, especially in today's mechanized world; but I've been wondering if my particular brand of sensitivity didn't start with dogs, or to be exact, with one dog.

I feel I ought to tell someone about this, get it off my chest. Of course it's too late to make right the damage but I can at least come clean.

Maybe if I take a deep breath and just blurt it out. Get it done before I have time to change my mind. Start by saying we'd moved from our old house on Cunard Street and were living in the upstairs apartment of a two-story building my mother and father and myself and I'd always wanted a dog but my parents were against it though I'd had a few cats talked them into letting me have a cat but not a dog not until I was twelve years old and that's when I got Rex I'll get right to the part that hurts or maybe I'll begin earlier on where he came from his name was Rex it wasn't a name I gave him I don't know what I would have called him but he already had a name he belonged to the people in the apartment downstairs a young Air Force couple with a little girl and they kept the dog in the back three-storey shed attached to our building it was part of the building and had rough wooden steps going down from our apartment to the cellar level and they the Millers were in the middle and they kept Rex there he was just a pup and he never got out and so he shit all over their part of the shed and on the stairs and they really didn't want him anymore and were going to have him shot and when I learned this I begged and pestered my mother until at last she gave in and said I could take him but I'd have to take care of him feed him and take him out for walks and so on but she wouldn't have him in the shed crapping all over the place and barking and scratching at the door and chewing stuff we kept there old clothes and shoes and boots and things our storage place into pieces and I said yes yes! to everything overjoyed to have my own dog at last like Lassie Come Home and all the dogs in the movies and books and that boys always had to be real boys their faithful companion man's best friend to go running jumping with me and fetching things and attacking burglars and heeling and sitting on command and it was going to be great though my cat didn't like him he was terrified of my cat the first time my cat who didn't have a name just the cat saw me patting Rex on the head he flew at him jumped on his back and was scratching and biting him and terrifying the poor dog I had to tear the cat off but he kept coming back and Rex whining and cowering and finally I had to grab my cat that I loved too and throw him hard against the wall and then he stopped picked himself up slunk away and I felt really really bad for doing that to him and because I thought they'd be friends I never expected that was going to happen and that hurts too it still does I think I'm one of those people who feel more for animals than people except for real little kids who are like animals anyway in their innocence and trust and so with all this Rex had to be kept in the cellar an old cellar with rough stone walls and a dirt floor the furnace down there and a room for coal and a small water-heating stove for the summer some wood to get the fires started a wood pile two small dusty windows cobwebs a large dark cellar with piles supporting the floor above we lived on the second floor as I said with the Millers on the first floor and the office of the doctor who owned the building on the first floor too off the hallway when you came in the front which he used this hallway for a waiting room and there was a door to the cellar leading off this small hallway waiting room as did the front stairs up to our apt I'm getting to it now the problem the problem was Rex wouldn't stop barking and he disturbed the doctor's patients and the doctor complained to my parents that was the root of it all keep the dog quiet or get rid of him that's what they told me so I had to keep him quiet I didn't want to lose my dog he was a black mongrel with a long snout we used to let him out on his own at first you could do that in those days dogs running free all over town it was before leashes were invented or might as well have been and he'd go across the street to a canteen run by Joe Moar that sold french fries with vinegar and salt and ketchup and Rex would go over there and hang around and stick his nose into the empty french fry cones and Joe laughed at first and said that's how he's got his pointed snout from sticking it into those cones but then he said Rex was becoming a nuisance bothering the customers jumping up on them and begging for handouts don't you ever feed that dog he said to me once and I said yes we feed him scraps like everyone else we didn't buy dog food hardly anybody did in those times we fed him leftovers and sometimes I'd get bones and scraps from the butcher's at Loggie's grocery store and so Joe Moar complained and we had to keep Rex at home in the cellar I was going to school it was winter and we couldn't keep him outside day and night in the freezing weather in the back yard and my mother didn't want to be bothered with him anyway the back yard was three floors down our bldg was on a hill the cellar was on ground level at the back and we'd have to put him on a rope and take him in and that kind of thing and Rex didn't have a collar anyway we couldn't afford money for unessentials like that so he was in the cellar barking and barking and if I wanted to keep him I'd have to go down to stop him so I'd go down and get him stopped but soon as I left him to go upstairs he'd start again it was a hell of a place to keep a dog black as night down there that huge cellar with ashes and rubbish stacks of boards old window frames doors screens pieces of furniture junk of all kinds just an unshaded light bulb hanging from a cord near the furnace which you'd switch on and off at the top of the wooden cellar stairs I was told to train him teach him not to bark stop him from making such a racket either that or he'd have to go and it's what I tried to do teach him in the way I'd been taught at home and in school and by older guys which was to toe the line or get a boot in the arse the Pavlovian system if he barked he'd get beaten smacked and talked to and once he was got quiet I'd make it up and pet him but he didn't learn he became scared of me so many times I came down to hit him and he started hiding I'd hear him barking and go down worried they were going to do it this time my mother exasperated warnings from the doctor landlord and I'd be angry and open the cellar door and I wouldn't be able to find him I'd call him and at first he came with his tail slightly wagging sidling up to me cautiously he had such a sad pathetic face huge moist brown eyes looking up at me I see his face perfectly today that's what hurts but I was so mad then I'd catch hold of him and hit him and as he whimpered I'd pet him feeling sorry for him then letting him know I really loved him if he'd just behave and then he stopped coming when I called him knowing what was in store and I'd hunt him down frustrated trying to find him in the dark side of the cellar tripping over things I'd hear him move and throw pieces of coal at him terrorizing that poor creature even more and when I caught him it was the same thing over again he had a rotten life right from the start from the Millers getting him as a pup for their little five-year-old girl who treated him like a stuffed animal dragging him around by one leg or by the ears they kept him in their back shed and never took him out and he shit all over the place down there it was good having him at first I'd take him out with me and we'd run together and roll in the snow and he was happy then then he ended up in the cellar alone in the dark and never knowing what I'd be like when I came down if he was going to get fed hunted beaten petted in the end he was totally cowed and one day I came home from school and he was gone my mother didn't want to tell me what they'd done she didn't want to lie but she didn't want to tell me either trying to find a way around it they hadn't told me what they were going to do just did it and however it was done nothing said about who came and took him and that he'd been put away as it was called put down put to sleep it was never said just that the doctor had had enough and he owned the place and the dog couldn't be kept anymore but when she knew I knew what they'd done she didn't deny it and I didn't understand felt betrayed I still thought I could have trained him in those times all the parents beat their kids it didn't mean they didn't want them it was how it was done I'd had my share of beatings more than I could count only Rex couldn't seemed to get it and he shouldn't have been in the cellar in the first place but there was nowhere else for him I was really sad despondent and over time ashamed of myself the way I'd treated him seeing his confused and frightened face I'd always wanted a dog one of the first books I'd had read to me had been "Lassie Come Home" I thought having a dog would be like that but it wasn't...

HOW LITTLE IT ALL MATTERS IN THE END

It was 1966 in Montreal, and I was watching an Expos ball game on TV, when the phone rang. A female voice said, "Who's this?"

"Who's this yourself?" I said.

"Hello."

"Hello."

"Is this Ray?"

"Yes. Is that you, Rebecca."

"Yes. I didn't know who you were."

"How could you call me if you didn't know who I was?"

"I'm off work today because of the holiday. Can I read you some poems I wrote?"

"What holiday? It's not a holiday."

"It's a Jewish holiday. Yom Kippur."

"You're a Jew?"

"A Jew-*ess*."

"All right, a Jew-*ess*?"

"Yes, but I'm not religious. I only observe the holiday because my parents do. I took the day off to please them."

"That was nice. Just a minute, I want to turn the TV down. Okay. What does having a day off have to do with not knowing who I was?"

"I found your number while I was unpacking. I didn't know whose it was and thought I'd dial and see. There was just the number and no name."

"What were you unpacking?"

"My things."

"Why were you unpacking your things?"

"Because I had the day off work. It gave me a chance to move back in with Jimmy. I thought we should get back together again. Do you want to hear my poems?"

I gave up trying to follow her tortuous line of thinking.

"Are they long poems?" I said.

"Not too long."

"Well, go ahead."

Her first poem was about a Roman legionnaire who was fighting Hannibal's troops. The army happened to be passing through a province where the legionnaire was from and he was given the day off to visit the old farm he'd left behind when he'd been called up to fight. It was Sunday, and he sat on a rock and looked around, and thought about his girlfriend.

"Do you like it?" she said. "It's about me."

"You're the girlfriend?"

"No, the legionnaire."

"It must have been in one of your previous lives."

"It must have been."

"You were a man back then, were you?"

"I still am. I'm everybody, man, woman, child. I'm everybody and everything."

"That covers a lot of territory." I had to laugh, but she didn't laugh with me. If we'd been talking in person she would have looked at me without expression, waiting for me to stop. The only times she ever laughed was when nobody else knew what was supposed to be funny.

I couldn't make much out of her second poem, which seemed to end with the lines:

and do nothing all day
but pull on their rods.

I asked her to repeat the ending.

"Did you say *rods?*" I asked.

"Yes."

"Do you mean rods, like their...?"

"You know, their penises," she said.

"That's what I thought."

She explained the poem was about young men who have no talent or purpose in life and so centre everything on sex.

"What about yourself?" I said. "Do you have a purpose in life?"

"I don't know. My life's unstable. I don't know whether to get married or stay single. I want children, but I believe in the equality of women."

"What's that got to do with marriage??

"Well, in marriage a woman is reduced to slavery."

"Oh? What makes you think that? It can be as easily the opposite, the man who's reduced to slavery. I know my old man worked six days a week and gave his whole pay cheque to my mother. Not that she had it great either, but she was no more slave than he was – they were both slaves, to hard times and low wages. And by the way, why is it a tiny woman can push a big man around, as so often happens?"

It wasn't just that, she said. Her dilemma was, she wanted a family, and yet she wanted to be free to do the things she liked without the responsibilities of a family. It was such a conflict it made her feel out of sorts.

And with that she hung up.

❖

Jimmy, by the way, was a sort of Renaissance Man, trying his hand at pretty much everything in the way of artistic creation. In his time he painted a few Abstract Expressionist paintings, wrote a few Neo-Expressionist Concrete poems, sculpted a few Post-Abstract Impressionist sculptures, composed a few Impressionist Neo-Abstract Concrete songs, took a few Post-Concrete Expressionist photographs, and so on. On occasion he worked as a printer's assistant, but having a creative mind he found practical matters difficult to concentrate on, and so it was never long before he got fired. Most of his income came in the form of handouts from his father who owned a small corner grocery store and from social assistance.

And so the years went by, thirty of them. Over that time Rebecca continued to break up and get back together with Jimmy, the two living on the artistic fringes of society and producing nothing of any note. Eventually Jimmy got sick, and for a time, near the end, she took care of him.

A friend who visited the apartment said, "It was like a scene from some macabre Russian short story. Chairs with three legs, vomit on the floor, Jimmy lying on a couch stiff as a board from Parkinson's disease, mouth hanging open, drooling. What a way to go."

She moved out again a few weeks later, leaving him for others to take care of, and this time never went back, other than for the funeral, which took place shortly after.

By then I was living in New Brunswick and so wasn't able to attend.

❖

I might mention that during her phone call that day so long ago I missed the Expos big inning in which they scored six runs to win the game.

THE CURSE OF VERA PETTY

I can remember Creighton Hancock as a young man, when his self-confidence was as solid and unshakable as the walls of the Bishop's Palace. Some might have thought him arrogant, and perhaps he was; but like the ignorance of others, his arrogance was bliss.

If you'd known him then you would scarcely recognize him today as the same person. He rarely speaks, indeed he's scarcely uttered a word in almost twenty years.

I'm sure he tries not to think about that night, but it must be like a spectre ever hovering over his shoulder, haunting him, mocking his silent futility. If you knew what it cost him you'd understand. All the expectant faces. Careers that hinged on the moment, where he had only to display some originality and agility of mind. Women he fell in love with and who waited to reciprocate, had he only spoken the words that sprang to his mind, but he couldn't. They died on the tip of his tongue, and with them went his hopes.

It was such a small incident, for the damage it did. But the ego is a fragile item. A tiny pin can burst a large balloon.

Let me tell you about that summer night so long ago.

He was at a dance in Chatham, and found himself dancing with a girl he'd never seen before. She was a very pretty girl and told him she came from Saint John. He asked her what her name was.

"Vera Petty," she said.

"Vera? One of my favourite names," he said. "What was your second name again?"

"Petty."

"That would be P-e-t-t-y?" he said, spelling it out.

"Yes."

With the band playing the old standard, *Smoke Gets In Your Eyes*, he whirled her skilfully over the polished hardwood.

"Petty. Well, I'm sure you're not petty. If you added an 'r' it would suit you better." He grinned, struck by a further inspiration. "While we're at it you might as well change the 'a' to a 'y' in your first name, and the next time I see you I could say: I remember you – you're *Very Pretty*!"

He drew back a little, waiting for the look of astonished admiration to come over her face.

Instead she sighed. "Yes, I know."

"You do? Oh, I see." He laughed. "You've heard it before. I guess every guy you dance with makes that remark."

"I'm afraid so." There was something in the way she said it, with an unmistakeable roll to her eyes.

"Hmm. And I gather everyone remarks that everyone makes that remark?"

She nodded.

"And does everyone remark that everyone remarks that everyone makes that remark?" He laughed tentatively.

"Oh yes. Always," she said.

"Really?"

"Really. And they use the same tone of voice when they say '*Really*'?"

For a moment he didn't know what to say. He said, "You don't have to do that. You're mimicking me."

"No. Well, I probably am, though I always say I'm not."

"That too?"

“Yes.”

He was normally a flawless dancer, but his sense of rhythm suddenly faltered and he committed the unforgivable sin of stepping on her toe.

“Oh, I’m sorry,” he apologized.

“That’s all right. It happens. In fact I’ve had a special pair of steel-toed shoes made.”

“Steel-toed shoes?”

“It’s very fine steel. You’d never notice.”

“Anyway, I’ll try once more,” he said, letting that one go. “So I suppose everyone remarks that everyone remarks that everyone remarks that everyone makes that remark... Am I right?”

“Yes,” she yawned. “But if you keep on you’ll reach the point no one has touched yet.”

“But,” he said, “the next man who comes along will go one better.”

“Yes,” she said.

“I gather everyone else has said that?”

“I’m afraid they have.” She glanced at her watch.

“And I suppose – but I can’t keep this up, I’m getting confused. I’d better quit right here.”

“I know,” she said.

“You mean...”

“Yes. They all want to quit here.”

“Well, I’ll fool them. I’ll keep going after all. I suppose that everyone has said that everyone else has said that everyone else has said that everyone else has said that – I mean about the next man coming along and going one better than what everyone has remarked about everyone else making that remark – But then I suppose everyone has tried to fool everyone else and kept going after all, and I suppose that... then... that..." He wilted.

The girl stifled another yawn. "Exactly," she said.

"For God's sake," he exploded. "Isn't there anything I can say original?"

"You can say what everyone else says in the end," she sighed. "But then it won't be original."

"Oh yeah? You want to bet? Well, try this one on. Go to hell! Go get stuffed! Go hang yourself! Go jump in the lake!"

She smiled patiently. "The very words," she said.

[This spoof was written in Montreal in the mid-sixties, when I was copy editor and chief staff writer for the tabloid newspaper MIDNIGHT. Since it was obviously a work of high literary merit I decided to accept it and publish it as a cover story in INTERCOURSE, the literary magazine I edited. I've since tidied it up a bit.]

WOLF POSES AS GRANNY – ASSAULTS GIRL

By O. M. Ghuse

Bartholomew Loop, 24, proved to be a wolf in grand-mother's clothing when he brutally molested little Rosa Hoode, a pretty ten-year-old redhead, in the woods near Grimmsville, N.B., earlier this week.

Police say the culprit, known locally as "Big Bad Bart", was only prevented from murdering his victim by the intervention of a passing woodsman who heard Rosa's screams and forced his way into the lonely cottage where the attack was taking place.

In the struggle that followed, the woodsman, 27-year-old Jamie Blithe, decapitated Loop with his axe.

Neighbours of the Hoode family say that on the afternoon of the crime Loop was working in the backyard of the house next door to Rosa's.

It was a hot afternoon and little Rosa was out on the lawn sunning herself, wearing only the bottom half of a bikini.

"I saw Loop staring over the fence at Rosa with his tongue hanging out," neighbour Mrs. Velma Voisin told this reporter, "but I didn't suspect anything, because she's only a child.

"I was aware he had a reputation. People said he was the type who stood on street corners leering and whistling at girls walking by and making suggestive remarks.

"I wasn't too happy hiring a man like him to rake the back yard, but I try to make a policy of not discriminating against people, if I can help it."

Mrs. Voisin said her husband was at work and her kids in school at the time and she herself was taking the sun in her yard, when she heard Rosa's mother call out to her daughter from the back door.

"Rosa, honey, will you take this basket of cookies over to your poor grandmother? You know how she's not feeling well."

"Oh, for heaven's sake, mother, it's too far," Rosa reportedly replied.

"Now, Rosa, don't be selfish."

"I don't want to walk away back there in the woods. I'm busy, can't you see."

"If you want to go picking plums with the little Horner boy tomorrow you'd better do as I say."

"His name is Jack. Really, mother, you're always making me do things."

According to Mrs. Voisin, as Loop listened in on the conversation his ears "literally perked up".

In a few moments Rosa went into the house and Loop returned to his raking. Suddenly he threw down the rake and said, "Mrs. Voisin, I just remembered I got to go see someone about something. I'll come back and finish up tomorrow."

Mrs. Voisin said before she could reply Loop threw down his rake and was gone.

"I didn't see which direction he took," she said. "I had the top off my bikini, and I didn't want to sit up and look for fear someone might see."

As Police piece the story together, Loop made straight for the forest with thoughts of laying a trap for little Rosa. He'd been raised in the area and knew that the widowed grandmother lived alone in a thatched cottage several miles from her nearest neighbour.

On reaching the unlocked cottage he walked in, and without pausing for formalities strangled the old woman and stripped off her nightdress and bonnet.

Then he stuffed the body under the bed and climbed into her clothes.

When Rosa arrived at the house he was lying in bed with the blankets piled up to his chin and the bonnet wrapped well around his head.

"Grandma, are you there?" Rosa called out, opening the front door.

"I'm in here, my little lovie-dovie," a voice relied.

"It didn't sound like grandma," Rosa later told police, "but I thought it was a sore throat or something making her voice sound hoarse."

Rosa went into the bedroom and took off the hooded coat she was wearing. She noticed her grandmother licking her lips.

"Grandma, what's wrong with you?" she said.

"Nothing, honey, I'm just fine."

"But you look so different... so strange. Have you been taking the right medicine?"

"Ain't nothing wrong, sweetie. I'm just sick, that's all."

"Little did I know how true *that* was," Rosa later said.

"But your eyes, they're all bloodshot. And you're staring at me in such a funny way."

"It's them medicines the doctor makes me take. Now come a little closer, dearie. I want to get a better look at you."

"Your voice is so rough."

"It's just a cold I picked up. You know how drafty it gets in this old house at night."

"And you haven't shaved today. I didn't know you shaved, grandma?"

"Heh! heh! Don't be afraid, I won't hurt you."

"And what big ears you have!"

"Hey, you don't have to get insulting. My ears ain't that big."

"I didn't mean to hurt your feelings."

"Alright then. Now come on and sit on the bed, why don't you."

"But, grandma, your mouth looks so much bigger. It used to be all toothless and shrivelled up."

At this point Loop winked, and snickered leeringly. "All the better to eat you with," he said.

"Grandma, you sound really sick. What's that leg sticking out from under the bed?"

"That's your old granny's leg, honey."

"Grandma's leg? But... but then who are you?"

"I knew all along something was wrong," Rosa later told authorities, "but I was playing for time. Anybody could see he wasn't my grandmother."

"Just call me Bart – Big *Bad* Bart!" And before she could move he jumped out of bed and caught hold of her.

"It was horrid," Rosa said after. "He threw me on the bed and made my lie there while he took off grandma's nightie. He didn't have a thing on underneath. It was disgusting!"

With a lupine grin Loop contemplated his perverted assault, leering, panting, slavering, whistling, readying himself to subject Rosa to every sexual depravity imaginable. As he bent closer the little girl screamed at the top of her lungs and clawed at his face to keep him away.

"Stop that bloody racket, somebody's gonna hear you!" Loop said. "Cut it out!"

When Rosa refused to be quiet, Loop wrapped his long fingers around her neck and began squeezing.

"I warned you, you're gonna get it now."

"I thought for sure I was a goner," Rosa later said. "He was just too strong, and I was waiting for my life to pass across in front of my eyes the way it's supposed to."

Fortunately at that moment there happened along a young lumberjack with an axe on his shoulder. Hearing the screams he ran into the house and confronted Loop and Rosa as they struggled on the grandmother's feathered bed.

"Here now! I say, what do you think you're doing to that little girl?" said the woodsman, whose name was Jamie Blithe.

Loop unwrapped his hands from Rosa's neck, glared up at the interloper, and said: "Who the devil are you?"

"That is not the point," replied Blithe. "Unless I'm mistaken, you're taking unfair advantage of this poor child, and I insist you stop."

In a rage Loop sprang to his feet and rushed at Blithe. As Rosa screamed shrilly, Blithe swung his axe and with one blow sliced Loop's head off and sent it bouncing into the corner.

"Gracious me!" exclaimed Blithe. "I think I'm going to be sick."

Rosa got to her feet and was fumbling around for her clothes. "My new dress, it's ruined!" she cried. "He ripped it and now you've gone and splattered blood all over it. Mother's going to kill me!"

"I say. Is that someone's leg?" said Blithe.

"It's grandma's. I suppose I'll have to wear something of *hers*. It's bound to be way too big."

She found a flower-pattered frock in the bedroom closet and put it on. Then she helped Blithe pull her grandmother out from under the bed. The old lady was stone dead and nothing could be done for her.

"I suppose we ought to call the police," said Blithe. "I didn't mean it, really I didn't. I was trying to get out of the way and – I think he hit my arm, didn't you see him? I'm sure that's what it was..."

But he needn't have worried.

"Clearly an act of self-defence," said Detective Inspector Alfred Hogget, in announcing that no charges would be laid against Blithe in connection with Loop's death. "He did the only thing he could under the circumstances. If anything he deserves a medal."

"Bless me, it was nothing, nothing at all," Blithe later told reporters. "It happened so suddenly. That terrible man running at me without a stitch on and quite unprotected. I shudder to think what he might have done had I not been prepared.

"I can't tell you much more. It was nauseating, all that blood and everything. I've been simply shattered ever since. I just know I'm going to have nightmares."

At her home Rosa expressed her satisfaction at having escaped a fate worse than mere death. "I owe not only my life but my virginity to Jamie Blithe," she said, "and I want to thank him for it. He's a real man and I hope to marry him when I'm older."

Her father, Stanford Hood, a local tanner and pet shop owner, gave the following statement to the press:

"Perverts like Loop are no better than dogs. If I had my way I'd skin them alive and tan and dye and hand-tool their miserable hides and sell them like I would any other animal."

Montreal, 1966 / Fredericton, 2006

OF EARS AND OTHER PARTS

The New Brunswick Department of Education used to have an itinerant singing teacher on its payroll. He came to St Michael's Academy once when I was in the seventh grade, and my class and all the lower grades were marched down to the auditorium to hear him. He was a jolly kind of man. He stood on the stage in front of us and sang some songs, and then got us to sing along with him. One of his songs went like this:

Do your ears hang low,
Can you swing them to and fro,
Can you tie them in a knot,
Can you tie them in a bow?

A lot of the younger kids laughed, and the singing teacher beamed, putting his hand out to calm them. He got us to sing this "ears" song with him two or three times, so we could learn it well; and as we sang you could hear some of the girls break out in titters.

When the period was over we were lined up two-by-two and paraded back to our classrooms. On the way up the stairs I heard my friend Walshy singing in a low voice, but not so low that everyone around couldn't hear him:

Does your bag hang low,
Can you swing it to and fro,
Can you tie it in a knot,
Can you tie it in a bow?

Soon half a dozen other boys joined in, rougher boys who wouldn't normally take part of a singsong, and for a while I thought they might sing all the way back to class like the children in the movie "Inn of the Sixth Happiness". But then one of the nuns ran up and whacked the nearest boy on the head with her pointer and put an end to *that* nonsense.

MIRACLES

"Master, I am unclean."

"Verily, then, thou shouldst go home and take a bath."

On the subject of miracles, I've been wondering about Jesus Christ healing a withered hand right in front of everyone. Brain damage or a plugged artery or a bad kidney, certainly – any part that's hidden from sight – but a withered hand suddenly turning into a good one? You'd think a miracle so spectacular would convert Beelzebub himself. And yet the Pharisees thought so little of it they resolved to have *this man* eliminated. They were a tough audience, for sure.

The old Roman author, Suetonius, wrote about a famous miracle in his book, *Lives of the Caesars*. I forget the emperor's name now, it may have been Augustus, but whoever he was, he was said to have cured a man of blindness by *spitting in his eye* ("touching his eyes with spittle"). What the audience there thought I don't know, but for my money that feat wasn't nearly up to restoring a withered hand. The man this emperor cured could have been a plant – he could have faked his condition; whereas the withered man couldn't have faked his shrivelled hand and sudden transformation, not in those days before stage magic.

What set me thinking about miracles was a radio program I happened on the other night. I was looking for some good music to listen to and idly turning the dial when the following popped out at me:

"In Jesus's name I command blind eyes – SEE!"

"Oh Lord Jesus, thank you Jesus! I can see good! Thank you Jesus!"

"She sees!"

"Yes, Lord, I see!"

"Don't go away, sister. How do you see?"

"I sees good."

"Do you see me?"

"Yes, I sees you."

"How do I look?"

"You looks good. You looks fine."

"And what about this man? How does he look?"

"He looks good. Ha! Ha!"

The program was *Brother Allan of Miracle Valley,* and featured afflicted people getting up on a stage in front of a large tent meeting – the blind, the lame, the leprous, the cancerous, the dead – all looking to be cured by the Lord.

The blind woman thanked the Lord and Brother Allen and danced off the stage, and then a blind *man* groped his way forward. Brother Allan put his hand over the man's eyes and carried on a shouting commentary:

"Jesus, I know you can make this man see! Show us your love and your power! Give us a sign, let all the world know that those who walk in the path of righteousness shall be healed! Jesus, O Jesus! I *know* you'll make this man see! Brother, when I take my hand off your eyes you are going to *see*. Is that right?"

"I'se going to see," the blind man said.

"When I take my hand away, by the power of the Lord Jesus Christ you are going to *see*! Who's going to make this man see?"

"Jesus!" shouts the crowd.

"What's going to happen when I take my hand away?"

"I'se going to see," says the blind man.

"Jesus, O Jesus, give sight to this man. Our blessed Lord Jesus – Everybody pray that this man sees!"

"Hallelujah! Praise the Lord!"

When the man finally had his vision restored, the organ played, the crowd cheered gleefully, and Brother Allan shouted and sang a few lines of a hymn.

Then he did another blind man. It must have been sight night. This man was asked how he felt, and he replied: "All right."

"All right?" A slight pause. "*All right?* Praise Jesus! He feels *allllll right*! You feel right, brother?"

"Yes."

"He was blind and now he sees! Praise the Lord! Go forth, my friend. Take Christ in your heart and go in peace!"

It was near the end of the program (I'd tuned in late), and time for the grand finale. The organ blared and faded and there was the sound of running footsteps getting closer and the hard breathing of a man out of breath.

Brother Allan introduced him. "This man came here last night, crippled and on the threshold of death. And behold, Jesus cured him and he's been running ever since! How do you feel, brother?"

"I feels good," the man panted.

"He's been running ever since."

"I'se been running ever since. It's good to be cured!"

"This man was supposed to be dead in a week, I found him in a hospital in Los Angeles, the doctor pronounced him dying, he hadn't walked in four years!"

Everybody cheered and shouted. "Praise Jesus! Amen! Amen! Hallelujah!"

At the close of the program listeners were requested to show their support by sending in donations. "Remember, brothers and sisters, the Bible says: as ye give so shall ye receive! Yay, and whatsoever you give shall be returned to you a thousandfold! Help us spread the word of the Lord!"

They could also buy Brother Allan's book, *The Glorious Power of the Blood of Jesus,* and get a free subscription to his *Glad Tidings* magazine which this month featured an article on how Jesus would quit smoking if he had the habit.[1]

❖

Before closing, I hope these few humble reflections on miracles haven't hurt anyone's feelings. I'm not irreverent, believe me, and would never scoff at *real* miracles, which are common enough. I can readily say that this life of ours on earth is a great mystery to me. I have no idea where I came from or why I'm here or where I'm going next or which came first the duck or the egg (though my guess would be the duck). I know nothing comes out of nothing, and that I didn't create myself, with my eyes and ears and other intricate parts. I don't doubt for an instant there's a being operating under the name of God behind it all. And that it would be easy for Him to kill me and make it look like an accident.

[1] *This reminds me of an inspirational slogan I saw on a huge billboard in front of a pentecostal church along the Southwest Miramichi:* LIGHT UP WITH JESUS

THE TALL MAN

(A snapshot from the old Balmoral tavern, Montreal)

He was a tall man in his mid-forties, dark-haired and with good features, but shabbily dressed. He was sitting with a shorter man in the Balmoral tavern, and from their conversation it was clear they had known each other for many years, probably since boyhood. The tall man was telling the other about a new business he planned to launch, and how it would quickly expand from one end of the country to the other, and then down into the states, and overseas, and all the profits it would make in just the first year, and so on, and the short man, who'd been listening with an expression of ironical scepticism on his face, at last broke in and said, "Johnny, you're never going to do anything now. You're talking like you did twenty years ago. That was twenty years ago."

The tall man drew back, indignant. He started to protest, but the other interrupted him: "You're still a fast talker, Johnny – you don't want to let me get a word in – but talking never got you anywhere. I worked in the coal mines to support my brothers and sisters when my father died. I was only sixteen, but I worked, Johnny. It's not talk that pays the bills."

"I know that, Harold. Don't tell me about work. I've worked too, goddammmit, don't think I haven't worked. But I don't want to be just another slave toiling day after day for enough to eat. I want to make my mark – I want to be the best. If I'm going to be a bricklayer I want to be the best in the world. If you want to make a million you have to think like a millionaire. Don't be afraid to get off the beaten track and take chances."

"What work, Johnny? What work did you ever do?"

"All kinds. I worked the oil fields out west. And in the lumber mills down east. And – "

"What oil fields? What did you do in the oil fields?" The short man wouldn't let go, peppering him with one question after another and laughing at his evasive answers.

Finally Johnny said, "What is this anyway, Twenty Questions? I know what I've done, and if you don't believe me that's your problem. I have to take a piss."

While he was gone the short man got up and moved to another table where two other men were sitting, leaving his beer glass behind. The men shook his hand and when the waiter wasn't watching offered him a drink of lemon gin that one had inside his coat.

When Johnny came back from the washroom he sat down without looking around, as though nothing had changed. He finished his glass of beer and poured the inch or so that was left in the short man's glass into his own. He sat for a while, staring at the table top, then spit a mouthful of saliva on the floor and rubbed his shoe over it. Downing the last of the beer he stood up and holding his old black overcoat in one hand beckoned the waiter over. He gave the coat to the waiter to hold while he put it on. Then he strode out of the tavern.

THE HOLLYWOOD PERIOD

It was after a meeting and I was in Hagan's Cafe with a guy known as Roy the Writer who was telling me about a trip he'd made to Hollywood in the days before he got off the booze. There are quite a few vagabonds like him in the Fellowship, literary and artistic types and such, including of course myself. Interestingly enough I'd had that same handle, "the Writer", when I was in Montreal, but when I moved to this place it was already taken by the aforementioned Roy G.

It's the anonymity thing – you don't hear many second names, and people start getting identified the way they used to in the Middle Ages, by what they do or what they look like or where they come from. Like Syd the Sailor, or Big John, or Manitoba Mike.

At any rate here's the story in the guy's own words. You can make of it what you will. I know what I made of it when I heard it: I thought that it could have been myself he was talking about, since in my own wild oats days I was just as crazy if not worse.

He began by telling me about his first wife, Rose, who had the bad luck to hold down that position when she did...

At the time she and I were living in Saint John (he said). I wasn't broke, I still had most of twenty thousand dollars savings my father left behind when he died. And I didn't have to chip in anything for rent or food, none of that stuff, household expenses. Rose was working and wearing the pants and the boots around the house, and such being the case I thought it was only right she foot the bills. My money was in the bank for a purpose. It was there to collect interest and to draw on for special occasions, and it was my security, the wherewithal should the need arise for me to have to get out some day and fend for myself.

I drank with Rose's money as much as I could, but she didn't allow me enough for the type of escapade I was accustomed to. Once she saw I was off and running the handouts stopped and it wasn't long before I had to dig into the old bank account.

A remarkable phenomenon back then in the early '80s was the bank interest. It was up close to twenty percent, which meant I was earning something like four thousand dollars interest a year from my savings account. This in turn meant I could drink that amount of money without cutting into my capital. I had to cut into it *some*, of course, but generally speaking I was in pretty good shape financially.

The trip to California put me out a couple of thousand, but such was life. It was a loss I had to take. I wrote it down as a business expense – venture capital or something. Adventure capital. I was off to make my fortune in the movie industry. If the great books I'd written could be turned into movies I'd never have to worry about money again.

It was one thing to be Canada's least recognized author, and to have a modest inheritance in the bank. Those are two things actually, and they were all very well. But they weren't enough for a man of my insatiable ambitions. I'd been crying to myself because I wanted to run away to Greece and find the woman or women of my dreams and live in a sunny villa by the sea. There was an ache in my soul for this (this panacea, this delusional answer to all my problems) and I couldn't have it. I knew what would happen if I tried. I'd get drunk and stay drunk and get lost and lose my money and be sick and terrified and within a week – using my credit card, if I hadn't lost it – I'd be aboard a plane home, shaking and on the verge of death.

And yet I was dying to go somewhere. It was almost inconceivable, how boring and unfulfilling my life was. Day after day of the same old nothing. I'd be dead before long without having lived, not really, not to the hilt. Sitting by the window watching life pass me by. Regrets about the opportunities I'd missed, the wrong choices made. Freighted down by a huge sob inside me, a mammoth bulbous teardrop at the base of my belly.

I had to go somewhere, that was all there was to it. I told Rose I thought I'd go to California. She said that would be nice. She didn't care what I did. She was all for it if it got me out of her hair for a while.

Although, even though I say it myself, I believe she still cared for me. I think she did. She was sticking in there pretty loyally, in her fashion, could still see some redeeming elements in me, a couple of minor things. She was the motherly sort, and she had no kids, so I suppose I was good that way. I was the troubled little boy. Troubled and troublesome. But nice when I was nice, or at least I used to be. Back in the good old days, those days of wine and roses, before I went to the dogs. They would keep a woman in the game a while longer, in memory of the good times.

And who could say for sure? I might pull out of the slump I was in. I'd only been sinking for the past ten years or so. You shouldn't give up hope that easily.

So it was off to Hollywood to call upon an old drinking mate from college days who was now a movie actor. The celebrated Harmon Cody.

❖

My best memory of California is of a flower in Harmon's garden. I don't know what it looks like or what it's called, but it has a perfume you could measure by the pound.

I'd sit inside this fragrance early every morning, flowers and greenery all about me, and do my daily meditation, which involved the first half dozen beers of the day to get the wrinkles out of the sails and the old ship under way.

My travelling companion Mooney didn't give up drinking or anything, he always had something in his hand, but somehow he was able to keep a rein on himself. Don't ask me how he did it.

I think he'd made up his mind before we left that he wasn't going to be the talk of Hollywood. Like me Mooney had been at St Luke's University with Harmon, we were all from the same class. And the two of them had been on the football team together.

I had started out in my freshman year playing football (I'd been a high school athlete) but the next year I quit because, having evolved into a renegade and general misfit, it was one of the things I had to do, break old ties. Harmon on the other hand had never played sports, unless you counted eightball or poker, but then he suddenly took up football because the coach saw this rangy tough-looking individual and envisioned him as a defensive end and asked him out to practice.

Harmon in his heart wanted to be wanted, like all of us, so he went, and ended up becoming one of the mainstays of the team.

That was all right because it was different, an ironic turn of events, and he didn't lose any prestige over it. It was like in the movies, the mean kid going out for football and becoming a hero. "Gee, he's really not such a bad guy after all, once you get to know him."

Mooney was always on sports teams, he was the centre on the football team and a defenceman on the hockey team. But he had other dimensions besides being an athlete. He was a well-rounded individual, a type of renaissance man with a big belly, a secret love of literature and the makings of an alcoholic. So we always got along.

The next curious place Harmon turned up was on stage at St Luke's year-end review. He was part of the can-can chorus line, dressed up like a Toulouse-Lautrec lady and doing a terrific high kick. Even though he was only one of a dozen or so in the line-up he stole the show. He out-pranced and out-capered and out-kicked all the others. And knowing it was Harmon, that itself was enough to bring the house down.

He was long and lean and when he wasn't laughing had a kind of slit-eyed menacing look about him. One night he and I and another fellow, Paddy Sheehan, were up river in the town of Wakefield drinking and looking for women when a gang of Wakefield boys surrounded us to see what we were doing there, college boys never being welcome in Wakefield. There were at least ten of them. There were some words passed back and forth and then they began crowding in closer, closing in on us. Paddy was just a little fellow, and I could see his face turn a pale green, and I probably wasn't doing much better. I was trying to think of something to say to lighten the atmosphere without losing face, when I heard Harmon say, "So you want to fight, do you? Which of you wants to fight? You bunch of fucking cowards." And without waiting he grabbed one of them and gave him a ferocious knee to the nuts. It was so sudden we were all left gaping, the Wakefielders, Paddy, myself. As the guy bent clutching at himself, Harmon drew back and ploughed him with an uppercut that knocked him flat on his back. Then he looked at the others, and each one he looked at backed off, none of them wanting to be next. They all edged away, muttering about the guy on the ground having it coming to him, being the type who was always shooting his mouth off, and about they themselves having nothing against college lads, they had good friends down there at St Luke's, and so on. Muttering their farewells.

I reminded Harmon of this when I got to Hollywood. He looked a lot different: hair greying at temples, shiny capped teeth with none of the spaces they'd once had, a calm maturity about him. You wouldn't know it was the same guy.

"It was great how you handled that mob," I said. "You were a tough guy back then."

"Tough? I wasn't tough. I was scared shitless."

"Go on! You sure didn't look it."

"How do you think I make my living today?"

"Ah. I see. You were acting."

"You're damn right."

After St Luke's, about six years later, he showed up in Montreal wandering the streets without a cent to his name. He said he'd taken up acting and was looking for work and wondered if I might be able to put him onto something.

It happened I had just quit my proof-reading job at the Montreal Star and was leaving for Europe next day. I didn't have any theatre or movie connections, but some friends were throwing a going-away party for me, and I took him along and introduced him. He was given a cordial reception, and a lady poet "of a certain age" offered him a place to stay for a few days. When I returned from Europe three months later he was gone.

Those were my peak years, back then in Montreal. His were yet to come.

When next I heard of him I was in the Maritimes and he was in

Hollywood. And some years after that Mooney got hold of his phone number and gave it to me.

❖

Mooney lived on the North Shore and was a freelance journalist and photographer, selling stories and photos to newspapers and magazines, mostly around the Maritimes. One of his justifications for our little junket was to write a story on Harmon and sell it to a magazine thus getting the money to repay me for his airline ticket.

Or maybe that was my idea.

At any rate there wasn't enough sobriety around to do anything so sensible as an interview and remember it. But he did take some photos of Harmon.

It was interesting to watch Harmon being photographed. Like a fashion model he ran through one pose after another, cocking his head at this and that angle, careful to show us his best side. I guess when you're an actor it's what you have to be able to do. Preen like a cockatoo, strike attitudes, not give a shit what the boys think. Quite a change from back in the rough neighbourhood in Halifax where he grew up.

Mooney was on his best behaviour, as I said. Images of him pop into my mind, and in every one he's laid back on a chair or a couch or a chaise or a bar seat and keeping his mouth shut as much as he can, grinning and chuckling and letting me do all the damage.

He must have planned it out ahead of time, prepared himself down to the last muscle restraint, rehearsed for hours. *Go slow now – take it easy – watch yourself!* – pounding it into his psyche – *be good!* Because it's not everybody you know who's turned out to be a famous movie star, and you'd like to be able to casually drop his name from time to time ("Oh, by the way, I was down to Hollywood to visit Harmon this summer? You know, Harmon Cody, the actor, he was in – "). And all you have to do is get drunk and piss on his carpet and rip the dress off his girlfriend for him to become just another guy who kicked you out of his house.

So Mooney must have buckled down and made a pledge to behave himself before we left, and miraculously stuck to it, passing himself off as relatively normal human being.

It was really too bad because I was accustomed to holding him up as an example of a guy with a drinking problem that was worse than my own.

Also, you know, I was paying his way, so he might have shown more consideration. Being alone in the spotlight might be considered desirable in a place like Hollywood, where two stars together is a crowd. But in the realm of the disreputable it gets lonely when you're the only one.

❖

The trip began on a promising note. The idea was, I would buy the return tickets, which were eight hundred dollars each, and Mooney would reimburse me from the sale of his story about Harmon (which as I mentioned earlier he never wrote, and so never felt a moral obligation to make the reimbursement). It was a typical binge investment of mine. When a drinking man's drinking he's a man of great wealth and distinction, and his money flows like wine and beer, while it lasts.

Having bought the tickets I drove up to the North Shore in Rose's car to pick Mooney up and bring him back to Saint John. And next morning after a few drinks for breakfast we took the plane to Los Angeles by way of Toronto.

Travel invariably stimulates my senses. On the flight to Toronto we kept the stewardess busy getting us those little airline shot bottles. I felt energetic, gregarious, lustful and free. In the Toronto airport, while waiting for our connection, I sat beside a delightfully pretty girl and engaged her in polite conversation. I've always been a brilliant talker when drinking, one of the finer conversationalists of our age, as Samuel Johnson was of his, when he was having a drop. The words flow with so little effort I can talk with my eyes shut or my hands tied behind my back. I'm even able to shift into automatic pilot and share in the pleasure of listening to myself! That's the best part. I especially love talking to the girls. I strolled up to this beautiful creature in the Toronto airport and sat beside her and introduced myself and helped her while the time until her flight to New York was called. I think she liked my Maritimer's simplicity, and the modest way I let slip that I was on my way to Hollywood to negotiate the movie rights to one of my books, and that I'd be staying with the movie star Harmon Cody who was a friend of actors like Paul Newman and Robert Redford, and that I'd be meeting all their director and producer friends and could probably get her into the movies if she was interested. I didn't need to tell her any of this, but it slipped out and after that there wasn't much I could do about it. I think she liked me anyway, because before she left she gave me her address and phone number.

We were in the month of June and I was wearing bluejeans and an old T-shirt which I'd cut the arms out of and a white denim jacket and cowboy boots. And I had a full beard and hair down to my shoulders.

After she was gone I looked about with understandable self-satisfaction, and still in an expansive mood turned to the chap on my other side and said, "Hi there, how ya doin'?" I'd seen this guy eyeballing the girl and trying to get the nerve, no doubt, to do what I'd come along and just done, and which he'd been staining to listen in on.

He was about thirty with hair cut to within a half-inch of his skull and he was wearing a plain brown suit and tie.

"Where're you headed for?" I said.

When he didn't answer I repeated the question.

He said: "Fuck you."

I raised my eyebrows.

"Just get the fuck away from me," he said, spitting the words through clenched teeth.

"What's eating you?" I said.

"You are, you hippy prick."

I was a little taken aback. Not a lot, since I was fairly well insulated, but still his words surprised me. "Do I know you? Have we met before?"

"I know you all right. I've seen enough of you around. So just get the fuck away from me, you long-haired freak. I hate your fucking guts."

I gave him a closer look. His face was twisted with barely-suppressed rage.

"Are you an American?" I said.

"You're fucking right I am. You fucking fag bastard."

"Then you better mind your tongue," I said, deciding to change my approach. "You're in Canada now, sonny." I glared back at him. "Up here we eat American creeps like you for breakfast."

The blood drained from his face. Smoke shot from his eyes. Froth gathered at the corners of his mouth. I thought he was going to leap at me, but with a mighty effort he pulled himself back. He was like a taut spring held rigidly under control.

He spoke in an undertone, hissing the words out so nobody else could hear. There were people sitting not that far away from us. "I told you, get the fuck away from me. I'm not telling you again."

"Oh, oh," I said, "my knees are shaking."

Our eyes were locked, each trying to stare the other down. After a minute or so I said: "You know, you're starting to get on my nerves. I think you need to be taught some manners. What do you say we take a little walk outside?"

He looked at his watch.

"What's wrong?" I said.

"You know what's fucking wrong. You know I got a plane to catch."

"Yeah, yeah. Sure you do."

His eyes blazed.

"You chicken-hearted pricks are all alike," I said. "You talk big but –"

"Fuck it!" he said. "Okay, cocksucker. Let's go." And he started to get up.

I didn't move.

"What's the matter?" he said.

"On second thought," I said, "why don't I introduce you to my friend over there? He'd be happy to tune you up for me. He could use the exercise." I nodded across the way towards Mooney who was as broad as he was tall, sitting back with his beefy arms folded across his chest. His hair was cropped like the American's and he was wearing a ballcap and a Moosehead Pale Ale T-shirt. Obviously not a commie faggot.

"Hey, Mooney!" I called. "This guy wants to meet you!"

A casual wave back.

The American's lip curled. "Fuck him, too. You don't have the guts yourself."

"I wouldn't touch crap like you. I've got too much respect for my hands."

"I'll remember you, buddy... If my plane wasn't leaving..."

The drink is a wonderful aid to courage. But cocky as I was, I'd seen enough movies to realize that your typical American carried a gun or a switchblade or some other deadly weapon on him, and I didn't relish the thought of bleeding to death in an airport alley. It also crossed my mind that the guy might be going to LA too, and on the same flight as ours! With visions of a homicidal crackpot on my trail I pulled back a little and said, in softened tones, "You should read your Bible and learn to love your neighbour. You'd feel better." And

leaving him with that Christian advice I rose to my feet and went over to where Mooney was sitting.

Mooney had been observing us. "Who's your friend?" he said.

I filled him in on the conversation. The American still had his cobra's eyes on me. Moon said, "You didn't have to let him know I was with you. He looks like a hit-man for the mob."

"I told him you were going to kick his arse all over Toronto."

The speaker announced a flight for Chicago. The killer got up and with a meaningful nodding of his head in my direction strode off. In our hearts we wished him good riddance. He was too serious a man for our liking.

The purpose of our voyage was not mayhem and murder. We sought the broadening of our horizons, as has always been the purpose of recreational travel.

❖

When the plane pulled into Los Angeles I helped a lovely darkhaired Spanish American girl with her suitcase and as we strolled towards the exit with her I told her about visiting our actor friend and that I was a famous author whose latest book was going to be made into a movie and my pal Mooney there was a renowned journalist who was doing a story on me for Esquire Magazine. I asked her to come along and join us, but she sighed and said unfortunately she couldn't, she had to catch a flight for San Diego. But she gave me her address and phone number. I felt an irresistible urge to kiss her and did so while Mooney gazed on in wonderment. She left laughing and waving and saying be sure and come and visit her. It seemed a good omen. Perhaps all the girls of California would be this friendly.

And speaking of California girls, Harmon was waiting at the airport with two of them. And a limousine with a uniformed chauffeur. After the initial salutations we piled in, Mooney and I on the main seat between the girls, and Harmon facing us on a smaller seat. The girls might have been twins, or at least sisters, they looked so alike (Mooney later described them as "book-ends"). Pretty things in mini-skirts and high heels, with long legs and other comely parts. They were actresses, Harmon said.

I started talking. As we drove I talked and when we got to his house I talked and I talked. Harmon and Mooney talked too, but not to the extent I did. It may have had to do with the fact I seldom spoke when sober, and had so much stored up to let out. The two girls didn't say anything. They chewed gum and looked bored. I tried some conversation on them but was met with vacant smiles and blank stares. Yawning, minds lost in space. Finally they looked at their watches and left. They were nice-looking, in a living-dead sort of way, but I hardly noticed them go. What did it matter? This was Hollywood! There were plenty more where they came from.

And there were. Harmon kept bringing girls over, or they'd drop in, and I'd talk at them a while. But again there was something missing: life, sparkle, intelligence. It was as if they'd all been hit on the head and never recovered. What we used to call stunned when I was a kid.

One even slept overnight on the couch.

I couldn't get up to try anything with her because by nightfall I got mighty sleepy and when I went under I was gone. Passed out, as it's known in some quarters.

The only girl I thought had anything on the ball was Harmon's ex-wife, Katrina.

I told him: "Now there's a woman, finally."

"She's my ex-wife."

"Oh."

So I had to forget about her. At least that's what I assumed, with my old-fashioned notions of honour and propriety, not wishing to offend my host, etc. I figured if she was coming to visit she must still be interested in him, and maybe they were thinking of reuniting. I told him they should, always ready with good advice, and feeling proud of myself for putting my friend's well-being above self-interest, especially since there'd be lots others like her still to come who *weren't* his ex-wives.

❖

Harmon wasn't yet a threat for an Academy Award, but he was landing character parts, supporting roles, and had done a lucrative TV deodorant commercial. From a financial point of view he was doing not too badly, for a guy who used to drink Hermit Canadian sherry out of the bottle with a couple of miscreants like Paddy Sheehan and myself.

We'd been rebels against the conformist establishment, we three, and he had gone on to become a movie star, and Paddy had gone on to go nowhere, getting himself killed at age twenty-one in a drunken car accident, and I had lived to become a literary legend, albeit an unnoticed one, ignored like Shakespeare and Cervantes in their day by critics and public alike.

Once, over the phone, Harmon had offered to buy the movie option on a novel I'd just had published, and I turned him down. I didn't want to take his money and have the guilt on my shoulders if a movie never got made. I said he could have the option for nothing. He said well, never mind, and didn't mention it again. I suppose he figured anything he was offered free must be worthless. Which, as it turned out, it was, from a commercial standpoint. He also invited me to come visit him. He had influential friends in Hollywood, he said, and would introduce me around, get a book or two of mine picked up for a movie perhaps, or find me a lucrative screen-writing job if I was interested. Follow in the footsteps of Fitzgerald, Faulkner, Capote and other literary celebrities.

At all events, and everything considered, when I got off the plane I had a fairly good standing in Hollywood, especially among the people who've never met or heard about me. Seriously, Harmon had shown some of my books to his friends in the "industry", as they liked to call it, and they had found them quite commendable, particularly the dialogue. I was a writer, and directors need scripts, and actors need characters to play, and lines to read, and a story to fit into, and all the other things that lead to an Oscar. So while writers in Hollywood are by all accounts at the bottom of the prestige ladder, they are still acknowledged to have a place.

Our first night at Harmon's went pretty much as expected. We all got drunk and there was a lot of whooping and roaring and laughter. Filling in the missing years and reminiscing about old college days and all that.

The next morning I was up with the roosters and out on the patio getting my medicine into me. It was my favourite time of day, when the going was right, and I was fit enough for it. Gazing around absorbing the rising sun and the foliage and flowers and sights and sweet scents of California. It reminded me of many early mornings from a former time, in the south of sunny Spain, the same type of earthly Paradise.

Mooney stirred a few hours later and joined me on the patio for a beer. And a few hours after that Harmon appeared. He was surprised we were out of bed already.

After he and Mooney had breakfast (unlike myself Mooney was an eating drinker) Harmon said, "Now, what would you like to see?"

He suggested a tour of the studio lots, MGM and Paramount and so forth... It was clear he considered this the ultimate thrill. Like the Mecca of our pilgrimage.

Being the perfect guest I let a groan escape me, and said, "Do we have to?"

When I was having a drink the last thing I wanted was to tour museums and cathedrals and monuments and movie lots.

I gathered it was his idea to drop us off at one of these studio lots and let us wander around all afternoon and then come back and pick us up when he was free. He couldn't accompany us himself because he had things to do. He always had things to do. Above all he had to talk on the phone. He had half a dozen telephones scattered around the house, some of them antiques (like his car and a lot of his furniture and assorted knickknacks and gewgaws about the place), and if he wasn't calling someone they were calling him. He had all that telephoning to do, and appointments with producers and so forth, and couldn't give us the tour himself; which of course made me feel neglected, on our first full day as his guests. And so I had another good reason for saying, "Do we have to?"

He seemed puzzled at my lack of interest. How could anyone *not* be interested in the movie-making world?

"Where do you want to go then?"

"Downtown. If there is a downtown. I heard there's no such a thing in LA."

"How about Hollywood and Vine?" said Mooney. "That's where the action's supposed to be. I'll bring my camera."

We climbed into Harmon's car, a mint condition Desoto from the forties. It was early afternoon and hot.

❖

There it was, the post with the signs on it. Hollywood going one way, Vine the other. Harmon let us off and we took a few turns, a little stroll up and down, gawking this way and that. We hadn't gone far when my eyes came to rest on a building advertising itself as *Frederick's of Hollywood*.

Every young voyeur knows about Frederick's of Hollywood. The ads on the back covers of Men's magazine of girls modelling sexy negligee. Send for the catalogue. Skimpy bikinis, transparent nightwear, panties with the crotch missing.

I'd been getting a bit sleepy by this time, having been up so early and all. Generally I had an afternoon nap when on a spree to prepare me for the night ahead. But the sight of Frederick's woke me up and put my imagination into gear.

I said to Mooney, "What we'll do is, we'll go in there and tell them we're in the market for a load of women's sex wear, only we need to see the product modeled. That's what these apparel houses are like, they keep half a dozen models on hand to strut before the customers, give them an idea of what they're buying..."

Mooney guffawed. He didn't believe I was serious.

"Where's your spirit of adventure?" I said. "Your *élan*, your *joie de vivre*, your *esprit de corps*? We could pull it off."

He continued to chuckle.

The problem was, he was controlling his drinking. He hadn't devoured enough yet for a man of his girth and capacity. He was still too inhibited by what's called good sense to have any fun.

He just wanted to walk up and down the street, he said. Soak in the atmosphere. Try out a few of the bars along the way. Take some pictures.

Well, there's nothing like someone's lack of interest to take the glow off a good idea. I was too fatigued to give him an argument. As soon as I saw he wasn't with me I got drowsy again. I was almost asleep on my feet.

In any case, with my eagle eye casting about, weary as it was, I'd honed in on another point of interest.

"Let me take your picture," he said. "Nobody's going to believe we were ever here if we don't have some evidence."

I posed for him beneath the signposts. And then I took a snap of him in the same location.

"We look like a pair of tourists," I said.

That's one reason I hate taking pictures in public. People see you and think you're just in from the farm.

"Time for a schnapps," said Mooney.

"Look, I've got to have a snooze."

"Here on the street?"

"No. There's a theatre over there. I'll go in and catch a few winks during the movie."

"What's on?"

"*Deep Throat.*"

Another snort of amusement out of him.

"I'm just going for the sleep," I said. "I can't help it what's on."

Everybody had read about Linda Lovelace and *Deep Throat*. They didn't show those kinds of movies back in the Maritimes. Maybe in Montreal the porn theatres were showing the real stuff, I don't know. But it wouldn't matter because I didn't live in Montreal.

"I'll meet you in an hour or so." I looked around. There was a bar a few steps away. "How about in there?" I said.

"Right," he said.

❖

To give some idea of the power of alcohol, I actually did sleep through the movie. All I caught were a few frames. I nodded off just as the doctor took his "instrument" out of her throat and began jackhammering her with it from behind.

Back home in the Maritimes, after a winter working in the woods, a man would hit the bright lights of a city like Saint John looking for a good time. He'd be looking for *women*. He'd spruce himself up and go calling, escort a young miss to the Church Social Centre where that evening *The Sound Of Music* was showing, featuring a few flashes of Julie Andrews's ankle. Ah, the excitement of glimpsing a finely turned ankle! The sweet romance, the shy blush on a maiden's cheek. Well, after a winter in the woods it wasn't enough – not for this lumberjack! I was off to California to take in a real movie. Find out what a woman looked like without her duds on. The bare facts beneath all those layers of skirts and slips and corsets and crinolines and bustles. And then, as I was on the verge of witnessing events worth writing home about, I fell asleep! It does indeed say something about the potency of drink.

It was intermission when I awoke. I was groggy, thirsty and restless, and hadn't the patience to wait around till the next showing. I had to meet Mooney anyway, if he was still waiting in that bar. So I withdrew down the dim aisle past a host of shadowy perverts and out into the blazing sunshine.

And it was hot, baking hot. The sidewalk was turning to jelly.

I darted across the street and into the bar. After the dazzling sunshine it was as if the lights suddenly went out. It was black as night in there. I closed my eyes and opened them and gradually shapes began to materialize. There was Mooney on a stool at the bar. I took the stool beside him.

"Jeez, this Coors is good beer," he said. "You ought to try one."

"I didn't know you liked beer." Mooney was normally a straight vodka drinker.

"Yeah, but this isn't bad."

"I'll have one later." I ordered a double gin and tonic, what I used for a wake-up drink, when I was feeling sluggish.

It was a dingy enough spot Mooney had led me to. A bar and a pool table and a few tables. Crud, slime and tobacco juice all over the floor. Windows covered, no light coming in from outside. A dull neon glow off the jukebox.

A swarthy Mexican chap was leaning on the end of the bar watching us. Pancho Villa mustache, round belly, eyes like the guy I'd conversed with at the airport. He had a pool cue in his hand.

He went over to the pool table and flicked on the overhead light.

Then he came up to us.

"Hey, man, you wanna shoot a game?"

Mooney said, "He's talking to you. I told him I don't play."

"Sure, why not?" I said. I tended to like games when out and about, and as a matter of fact was a better pool player drinking than when sober, for whatever reason.

"Okay," he said. "How much we gonna play for?"

"Oh," I said, "I don't want a money game."

"Come on, man. We don' play for nothing. Where the fuck you think you are? I saw you lookin' at the table. You're a pretty hot shooter, eh?"

"Who, me?"

"Don' give me that shit, man. Don' try to hustle me. We play a game for twenty bucks. Tha's nothin'. I wanna see how good you are."

"Aw, I don't think so. I'm not in the mood."

"Okay, we make it fifty bucks. I break the first game." He turned and headed for the table. I stayed put. He came back.

"Wha's wrong, man? You chicken?"

"I told you, I'm not in the mood."

"Fuck your mood, man. You come in here like some shit-hot asshole hustler. Who you think you're fuckin' with, man?"

"Look, I said I'm not interested, okay. I don't have time. You find someone else to play with."

It was like the airport character all over again. Only this time I knew better than to try bluffing. The guy wasn't that big but he was holding a pool cue and most definitely had a screw loose.

He gave me a look that said this wasn't finished yet, and calling me a fucking this and that went back to the end of the bar. I could see he was going to brood on how I'd insulted his manhood and his honour and that there was no choice for him but to cut my liver out.

"I don't think we should stick around here," I said to Mooney. "This bar has lost its charm." I downed my gin in two drinks, which was about right for a quick yet dignified withdrawal.

The other patrons were giving us the fishy eye as well. They were a vile-looking lot, sitting around with their red eyes glowing in the dark like a pack of rats.

We sidled out the door and into a shower of sunlight and sun-warmth, then tore off down the street before Pancho Villa could come after us.

Hollywood, the jewel of America, the glorious paradise everyone dreams of going to in this life and the next. Where you can walk into a bar for a quiet drink and come out with your throat cut and your liver extracted. If this was the national showplace what kind of shape must the rest of the country be in?

It appeared the movies and tabloids were right. Society down here was a jungle.

❖

Going to the beach was my idea. I hadn't travelled clear across the continent to miss having a dip in the Pacific Ocean. It was a day like the day before, hot and cloudless, as we loaded up our gear and climbed into Harmon's Desoto and sped off on our next escapade.

I'd been to beaches before, naturally, in Canada and Spain, but never to one like the beach Harmon took us to. Beaches can be crowded, but here the crowd went on for miles and miles, as far as the eye could see in both directions. There must have been more people on that stretch of sand than live in the entire province of New Brunswick.

We set down the beer cooler and spread out our blankets and towels and stripped to our bathing suits. Harmon and Mooney weren't interested in the water, being content to lie in the sun and tan. But by now I needed a swim, even if I hadn't wanted one, because my mid-afternoon sleepies were coming on, and the salt water was just the thing to wake me up. The great Pacific ocean looked beautiful, huge waves rolling in higher than a standing human and tumbling with a great splash in the shallows. With an extra big one approaching I waded out a bit and when it was almost on me gave a whoop and dove into its middle.

It was a force greater than I'd anticipated. I went tumbling and rolling and thrashing about for a lot longer than I'd bargained for. When I popped up out of the moiling water I was breathless and laughing. What a ride! I rolled to the top of a swell and looked around to see if Mooney and Harmon had been watching, and was surprised at how tiny everyone on the beach had become, like Lilliputians. And just as strange, where were all the other bathers? It actually took a moment to sink in that I was a long way from shore, however I'd got there. And then something else registered, a phenomenon I'd read or heard about, and I realized why I was where I was: I'd been caught in an *undertow* and carried about a mile out to sea. I can remember a sudden feeling of loneliness at finding myself distanced that far from the rest of humanity, and the only one of who might be drowning. And then I thought I'd better try swimming back in.

Fortunately the salt water was buoyant, and I had the tireless stamina of a man facing death if he flagged. And I think having a drink or two in me helped, kept me optimistic and free of panic. Although I wasn't conscious of it, there was a current or a tide out there as well, but it was running more or less parallel to the shore and not praise God westward to sea. It made the swim further, swept me along so that I had to come in at a forty-five degree angle; but I kept on until my foot felt bottom and I staggered ashore like a weary castaway.

I didn't know quite where I was, however. I hadn't as I said been aware of the tide carrying me, I thought I'd been swimming straight in; and in any event I'd been too preoccupied to think of landmarks, even supposing I could have picked one out in that Sahara of endless sunbathers. Once ashore that was still all I could see, hordes of humanity in bathing costumes lying and sitting and standing, towelling, oiling, strolling, trotting, tossing frisbees – and none of them Mooney or Harmon. I looked around, debating which direction to head in. I was lost, but being firmly on dry land, not worried, confident that in one way or another I could find my way, even if it meant asking some pretty girls in bikinis that my eye chanced upon. The two selected were true California girls, blonde, tanned and friendly, and as helpful as they could be without moving. They listened with amusement to my account of escape from the briny and suggested I ask a lifeguard for directions. I said it was a good idea, and settled down beside them, by now in no hurry to leave, seeing as how we were hitting it off so well. They were still in the sunbathing position, the pretty one on her back, the even prettier one on her belly, myself sitting beside them yakking away, when, as a man in my condition might do, I felt an irresistible warmth of affection for the two of them, and on impulse ran my fingers along the sun-burnished arm of the prettiest. And too late thought better of it. She gave such a start I thought she'd been stung by a hornet. She lifted a good foot off her towel.

"*Hey!*" she cried. "*What the hell do you think you're* – " Staring blue murder at me, her whole manner altered, as though suddenly seeing me for what I was. Oh, there was a great to-do, she was going to call the police, have me arrested and deported as a sex fiend, and I don't know what all else.

It was all because of the way you view life when you're half-loaded. You think others are travelling at the same speed as yourself, and in the same direction, seeing what you see, feeling what you feel, and are in a similar advanced and heightened spiritual and emotional condition. But the trouble is, unless they've been boozing themselves they aren't. And they can be greatly unappreciative. These girls wouldn't listen to my smoothing-over blandishments. I'd escaped the sea's depths to be met by the furies of Hell. They were all-out dead serious. I didn't know which way Harmon and Mooney were, but I picked the way that was handiest and made an inglorious retreat, bowing and scraping as I withdrew, saying I'm sorry, I'm sorry, no offense meant, the sun must have got to me, I was just brushing sand off your arm...

By pure chance I chose the right direction, for after some minutes of scurrying through the crowd I saw my friends approaching, looking for me. They of course thought I had drowned.

❖

It was around this time that the stream of women Harmon had been inviting over dried up. It more or less coincided with my wearing out my welcome.

Not that you could blame me for my behaviour; there were extenuating circumstances. It was the fault of the blackouts, mainly. To this day I don't recall half what I did. You can't blame a fellow for how he acted when he was in a blackout; I certainly wouldn't. I'd had these afflictions all the way back to my earliest drinking days, as a teenager, friends telling me things I said or did (and usually wished I hadn't) the night before, of which I had no memory. It's a common phenomenon among two-fisted drinkers, holes in the memory.

I remember Harmon took us in the evening to see a former mistress of his, a wealthy woman who was quite a bit older than himself, and from what I gathered a person of influence in the movie industry – someone who might be able to do things for me, he said. Her name was Eleanor, and as I recall we hit it off rather well, at first. She seemed taken with my wit, and was pouring me drinks and chatting me up, and when Harmon and Mooney rose to leave took hold of my arm and asked me to stay, and – and then I don't know what. Next thing I was at Harmon's and he was scolding me for having insulted the woman.

It was news to me. "Oh, you must be mistaken," I said. "I wouldn't do a thing like that. She obviously misunderstood me..."

"She was in tears when she phoned. She said she'd never been so humiliated in her life. I think you ought to call and apologize."

But how could I? What had happened? I'd gone there with Harmon after we'd all been to the beach, and he'd obviously left me with her, because if he'd stayed she wouldn't have had to telephone him later. And how did I get back? By taxi? I didn't remember that either...

You can't ask too many questions, because if you do ordinary people might get the idea you drink too much. They might think you're out of control and should quit the bottle altogether. And then where would you be?

From my past record, incidents in my career that I did retain, I knew I was quite capable of having asked the woman point-blank if Harmon had been a gigolo at one time, citing as evidence the fact he had lived with an old broad like her.

When drinking I like to speak my mind. It's one of the things I can't help about myself, and indeed I'm proud of myself when I do it. My rationale is that there's so much sham and hypocrisy in the world that it's refreshing when someone outspoken like myself comes along.

I truly believe this at the time, but I can assure you I don't have the same feeling next morning. Not until I get myself tanked up a bit and ready for another day of mischief.

Of course I didn't apologize to the woman. It wasn't possible when I didn't know what I said and couldn't admit I didn't know. Furthermore it wasn't in my nature to apologize to people, except for occasions like with those girls on the beach, when there was a chance I might get arrested. When you apologize it's the same as saying you were in the wrong, and when you're in the wrong you get a stick across your behind. At least I always did. It was how it was done in the old days.

❖

Harmon fancied himself a gourmet cook, and put his heart into cooking us up some scrumptious meals, none of which I ate. I could never eat much when drinking – a bit at first but as the rampage went on, virtually nothing. As most drinkers can attest, food and drink don't mix, although there are a few odd types like Mooney who seemed able to combine the two. At the beginning of a bout you avoid food because it takes the edge off the drink, dulls the glow; and later on you can't eat because food becomes repulsive. But you can drink! No problem there. While Harmon and Mooney ate, sipping their glasses of wine, I filled and refilled my wine glass and guzzled with a connoisseur's relish. It only took me a couple of days to clean out Harmon's bar – expensive wines, expensive brandies, expensive whiskies, expensive liqueurs, foreign beers, the works. After that he drove us to a liquor store where we stocked up again, filling the trunk. I wasn't being cheap, drinking his stock; it just happened to be there, ready at hand. I bought a great supply myself at this store, and the others bought some, each according to his needs.

❖

Harmon took us to see some of his friends at a mansion in the Hollywood Hills; important friends, including a producer named Sam or Jack or something, a bald-headed fat man who had read my books and was apparently interested and wanted to meet me. It was his mansion we went to. We went in the evening, which was a mistake. I'd been up and at the bottle since six in the morning, with just an hour break in early afternoon for a nap. I was in a good mood when we left, full of fun. As we were lounging around the pool on padded deck chairs having drinks (gin and tonic for me) and smoking fat cigars, I recall the producer being complimentary about my books, and suggesting I come see him tomorrow morning. And then somehow the conversation drifted away from me as its focal point and these prosperous and self-satisfied looking men began talking shop, going on about this property and that, and what star was doing what, monologing as though there wasn't a great guest author in their presence. The producer went to fetch a script to show Harmon – it was all sort of like a dream, an ethereal quality about it. I was slumped in my chair, reclining almost on my back, as was my custom when relaxing, and chuckling to myself as an idea took shape in my head. The producer returned and as he passed in front of me (honestly, I couldn't resist, the temptation was just too much) I drew back my foot and casually (as Mooney later phrased it) propelled him into the pool. He was fully dressed, Yves St Laurent silk shirt and blazer and ascot tie, Gucci shoes. The pages of the script flew through the air and rained down on his head as he surfaced splashing and fuming. The others all stared, looking from him to me, open-mouthed. Not a chuckle out of them, not even after he'd climbed out and stood dripping like an old walrus.

I didn't know what to make of it. Wasn't that what everyone did in Hollywood? The place was notorious for throwing people fully clothed into pools. I'd seen it in scores of movies, and it was in every account of a Hollywood party ever reported in the press. Our host ought to have enjoyed the prank, or at worst laughed it off. But he didn't, and neither did anybody else. Or nobody except Mooney, who was too discreet to let on until after we'd left. And we did leave, and in quite short order, the soaking wet man having made clear the party was over.

I told Harmon on the drive home it was a disappointing party anyway. Not one nymphomaniac starlet, when there should have been at least a dozen, all topless if not fully naked. There would have been some throwing of bodies in the pool *then*. And nobody would have got into a huff about it either. As for the producer fellow who no longer wanted to see me next morning, I wasn't worried. There must be plenty more where he came from.

"Oh?" said Harmon through his teeth. "You think so, do you?"

❖

Harmon was out and around doing whatever actors do between acting jobs. He was a great gadabout, which I guess is what you have to be to get ahead in the world, although it never helped me. I said to Mooney, "We can't just sit here doing nothing. Since Harmon won't find us a woman why don't we rustle up a couple of call girls and invite them over. It's on me." So I got out the yellow pages and looked under escorts and call girls and hookers and strumpets and whores and everything I could think of and there was nothing – not a single advertisement of the kind in the book. And this Los Angeles! I tried under "S" for Sex, under "L" for Lust and Love and Ladies of the Evening, and under "P" for Pleasures of the Flesh, and "B" for Bordellos, and "C" for Cat Houses – Finally I tried some numbers under models, and got coldly hung up on a few times. I was about ready to quit, when I reached a gentleman who seemed to appreciate what I was looking for. I assured him that I and my associate were Canadian businessmen and not cops and were just looking for a bit of fun, and could he send over a couple of his choicest? He was cautious, did a good deal of humming and hawing, but at length opined he might be able to fix us up, and where was my hotel? I said it wasn't a hotel and gave him Harmon's address. Oh, he said, that's a long way from here. I said, Don't worry, I'll pay their cab fare. Well, he'd try, he said. He'd see what he could do.

We were still waiting when Harmon returned and asked us what we'd been up to all afternoon. I said, "Nothing much. Right now we're waiting for a couple of whores to show up."

He almost went through the roof. "Whores! You're bringing whores here?"

"Why not? What's wrong with that? Look, we come all this way, we're in a city that's full of women and we haven't gotten laid yet. If you'd come to visit me I'd have set *you* up quick enough."

It was true, as I understood truth. In my imagination I could have done that. I'd have taken care of him in no time flat. I'd have flown Brigitte Bardot in, or Sophia Loren. And bought him a Rolls Royce while I was at it.

"What are you talking about?" he said. "I was bringing girls for you every day."

"Yeah, but they weren't – they weren't our type."

"What type? What was wrong with the two sisters I brought to the airport for you?"

"What about them?"

"Weren't they good enough for you?"

"Sure, but – "

"But what?"

"They weren't – Well, they had no conversation. They didn't say anything and then they left."

"How could they say anything? They couldn't get a word in with you around. You never shut up. It's not surprising they got bored and left. They got tired of being ignored."

"Oh."

"What's the number of those whores you called?" he said.

"Why?"

"So I can cancel them. You're not bringing whores into my house."

❖

I said to Harmon, "You have to give Hollywood its due, it's got sunshine and flowers and palm trees and lots of nice Spanish architecture. And I know there are piles of money to be made in movies. But weather and scenery aren't everything, and believe it or not, neither is money. First and foremost I have my integrity to consider. I have to live with myself. And so," I concluded, "I've decided not to sell out."

I told him this as we were packing, after he'd informed us it was time we moved along.

He said, "I'll call you a taxi."

"Aren't you going to drive us to the airport?"

He said, "All the way out there? Don't be foolish."

❖

These events took place back in 1981, during my first life. It wasn't until my second life (which began when I sobered up) that I was able to take another trip, going this time to Paris, where I stayed the better part of a year.

My reason for going to Paris was, I had always wanted to have a Paris period, like other famous authors, such as F. Scott Fitzgerald.

It was while I was in Paris that I was struck by an interesting contrast between Fitzgerald's career and my own. As the world knows, Fitzgerald's travels took him to Paris first and then to Hollywood, where he stayed on to write movie scripts; whereas in my case it was just the opposite. My itinerary took me to *Hollywood* first, and *then* to Paris. And I never wrote movie scripts. And another difference was, he died in Hollywood and I didn't. Although I probably I could have if I'd really wanted to.